Washington State Bed & Breakfast Cookbook

Look for the first book in the
Peppermint Press B & B Cookbook Series

Colorado Bed & Breakfast Cookbook

Here's what people are saying about the
Colorado Bed & Breakfast Cookbook!

"What a treasure! Two books in one — an excellent guide to the bed and breakfast facilities in Colorado, complete with drawings, as well as a collection of outstanding recipes."
— Wally & Linda Stephens, Publishers
NATION'S CENTER NEWS

"A unique regional classic! Functional design, beautiful to behold and a gourmet's delight. Love is this book's essence. Carol and Doreen loved doing it, you will love owning and using it."
— Suzanne Aikman
AUTHOR, RADIO HOST,
MEDIA PRODUCER

"Colorado Bed & Breakfast Cookbook is tastefully done, is just the right size, is a pleasure to use, and has wonderful recipes. A great and fun Colorado cookbook that belongs on everyone's cookbook shelf. It would also make a great gift."
— Ann & Fred Milenovich, Owners
THE BOOK RACK

"During holiday gift-giving time, it's a bonus to find a practical, yet pleasurable item that ... offers select recipes from and travel descriptions of 85 Colorado bed and breakfasts."
— Mary Southworth
DENVER CATHOLIC REGISTER

"Their book ... has run up unusually high sales. In about a year ... has become a regional bestseller."
— Brad Smith
DENVER BUSINESS JOURNAL

"... new local treasure."
— John Kessler
THE DENVER POST

Washington State

Bed & Breakfast Cookbook™

~

A SELECT RECIPE COLLECTION

~

From the Warmth & Hospitality of 85 B & B's and Country Inns throughout Washington State

~

Carol Faino
&
Doreen Hazledine

Peppermint Press

Denver, Colorado

Published by
PEPPERMINT PRESS
PO Box 370235
Denver, CO 80237-0235

First Printing   July 1998   10,000 copies

Cover Design: SYKES DESIGN GRAPHICS
                     Estes Park, Colorado
Cover Photo: HUDSON PHOTOGRAPHIC ARTISTRY
                     Bremerton, Washington
Front Cover Location: WILLCOX HOUSE COUNTRY INN
                     Seabeck, Washington
Author Photo: HUDSON PHOTOGRAPHIC ARTISTRY
                     Bremerton, Washington
Author Photo Location: SALTY'S ON ALKI BEACH
                     Seattle, Washington
Washington Map: TRUDI PEEK
                     Port Orchard, Washington

Library of Congress Catalog Card Number: 98-065469

Disclaimer and Limits of Liability
Recipes and descriptions of the bed and breakfast inns featured in this book are based on information supplied to us from sources believed to be reliable. While the authors and publisher have used their best efforts to insure the accuracy of all information at press time, the passage of time will always bring about change. Therefore, Peppermint Press does not guarantee the accuracy or completeness of any information and is not responsible for any errors or omissions or the results obtained from use of such information. The recipes chosen for inclusion are favorites of the inns and are not claimed to be original. Although the authors did not personally visit every inn, each recipe was home-kitchen tested, taste-tested and edited for clarity. This book is sold as is, without warranty of any kind, either expressed or implied. Neither the authors nor Peppermint Press, Inc. or its distributors shall be liable to the purchaser or any other person or entity with respect to any liability, loss, or damage caused or alleged to be caused directly or indirectly by this book.

Additional Washington bed and breakfast recipes may be found in *A Taste of Washington State*, published by Winters Publishing of Greensburg, Indiana.

Special bulk-order discounts are available on Peppermint Press books. Companies and organizations may purchase books for premiums or for resale, or may arrange a custom edition, by contacting the Marketing Director at: (800) 758-0803.

ISBN 0-9653751-9-6

Printed in the USA by

WIMMER
The Wimmer Companies
Memphis

To our
husbands,
Rod & Don,
with love

Acknowledgements

Creating a book is a work involving many people. We owe a great deal of gratitude to the following friends and family members for their support, inspiration, time and talents: Terri Hulett, Linda Faino, Gordon McCollum, Doris Anderson, Morgan Anderson, Margaret McCollum, Harold McCollum, Judy Cochran, Jeanie Rienhardt and Krista Flock.

A special thank you to the owners, innkeepers and chefs of the 85 Washington State bed and breakfasts and country inns who generously shared their recipes, artwork, enthusiasm and encouragement.

We want to express our love and heartfelt thanks to our parents, Margaret and Harold McCollum and Nan and Lawrence Kaitfors; our husbands, Rod Faino and Don Hazledine; and children, Kyle, Erin and Ryan Faino for their continuous support and encouragement.

Table of Contents

Introduction

Dotted amid Washington State's beautiful beaches, majestic mountains, thick forests, bountiful orchards and golden wheatfields, hundreds of unique bed and breakfasts and country inns await your visit.

Are you ready to be pampered by your hosts, to be enlightened by their knowledge of local history and attractions, to be stimulated by conversations with fellow travelers and to enjoy an unforgettable breakfast feast? Then browse through our book to choose a place that is perfect for you! With careful planning, you can experience a fun and enriching adventure and return home with memories that will last a lifetime. You can also create your own special memories at home by preparing and sampling the many tempting, mouth-watering recipes that have received "rave" reviews from the B & B guests.

Whether you are a newcomer to Washington State, a visitor just passing through, an annual vacationer, or a life-long resident, enjoy the *Washington State Bed & Breakfast Cookbook.*

Carol & Doreen
July 1998

To check out recipes and travel information on the bed and breakfasts and country inns in Washington State and Colorado — and to follow Carol and Doreen's next adventure in the Peppermint Press B & B Cookbook Series — click on their Website at:

www.bbcookbook.com

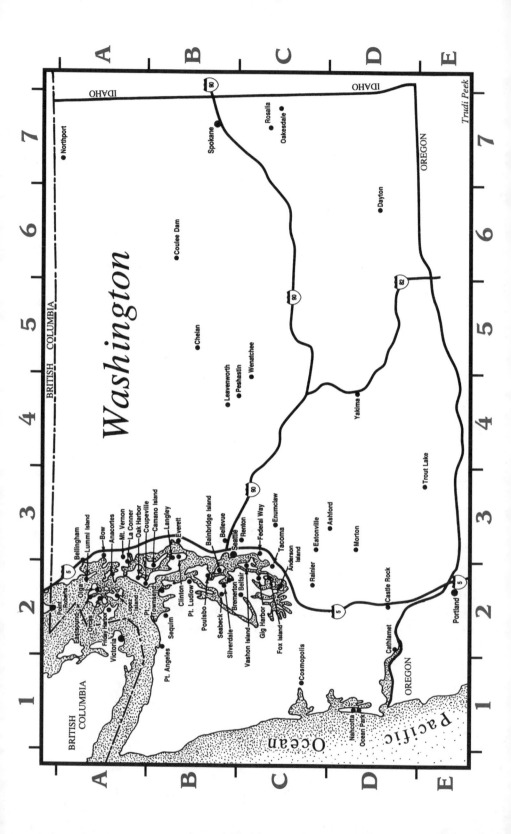

Washington

B & B Locations

Location	Name	Map
Anacortes	Outlook	A-2
Anderson Island	Hideaway House	C-2
Anderson Island	The Inn at Burg's Landing	C-2
Ashford	Growly Bear	D-3
Bainbridge Island	The Woodsman	B-2
Belfair	Selah Inn	C-2
Bellevue	Petersen	B-3
Bellingham	Bellingham's DeCann House	A-3
Bellingham	Stratford Manor	A-3
Bow	Benson Farmstead	A-3
Bremerton	Highland Cottage	B-2
Camano Island	Camano Island Inn	B-2
Camano Island	Inn at Barnum Point	B-2
Castle Rock	Blue Heron Inn	D-2
Cathlamet	Redfern Farm	D-2
Chelan	Highland Guest House	B-5
Clinton	Home by the Sea	B-2
Cosmopolis	Cooney Mansion	C-1
Coulee Dam	Four Winds Guest House	B-6
Coupeville	The Captain Whidbey Inn	A-2
Coupeville	The Compass Rose	A-2
Coupeville	The Inn at Penn Cove	A-2
Coupeville	The Victorian	A-2
Dayton	The Purple House	D-6
Eastsound	Kangaroo House	A-2
Eastsound	Otters Pond	A-2

3

Eatonville	Mill Town Manor	C-3
Enumclaw	White Rose Inn	C-3
Everett	Harbor Hill Inn	B-3
Federal Way	Palisades at Dash Point	C-3
Fox Island	Beachside	C-2
Fox Island	Island Escape	C-2
Friday Harbor	Arbutus Lodge	A-2
Friday Harbor	Duffy House	A-2
Friday Harbor	Olympic Lights	A-2
Gig Harbor	Harborside	C-2
Gig Harbor	The Pillars	C-2
La Conner	Katy's Inn	A-3
La Conner/Mt. Vernon	Ridgeway Farm	A-3
Langley	Log Castle	B-3
Leavenworth	Abendblume Pension	B-4
Leavenworth	Bosch Gärten	B-4
Leavenworth	Mountain Home Lodge	B-4
Leavenworth	Run of the River	B-4
Lopez Island	Inn at Swifts Bay	A-2
Lopez Island	MacKaye Harbor Inn	A-2
Lummi Island	The Willows Inn	A-2
Morton	St. Helens Manorhouse	D-3
Nahcotta	Moby Dick Hotel	D-1
Northport	Northern Lights	A-7
Oakesdale	Hanford Castle	C-7
Ocean Park	Caswell's on the Bay	D-1
Olga	Spring Bay Inn	A-2
Orcas	Chestnut Hill Inn	A-2
Peshastin	Lietz's	C-4
Point Roberts	Cedar House Inn	A-2

4

Port Angeles	Domaine Madeleine	B-2
Port Angeles	Tudor Inn	B-2
Port Ludlow	Nantucket Manor	B-2
Port Townsend	Ann Starrett Mansion	B-2
Port Townsend	Annapurna Inn	B-2
Port Townsend	Baker House	B-2
Port Townsend	The James House	B-2
Port Townsend	Lizzie's	B-2
Port Townsend	Old Consulate Inn (F.W. Hastings House)	B-2
Port Townsend	Quimper Inn	B-2
Port Townsend	Ravenscroft Inn	B-2
Poulsbo	The Manor Farm Inn	B-2
Rainier	Seven Seas (7C's)	C-2
Renton	Holly Hedge House	C-3
Rosalia	Country Inn Guest Ranch	C-7
Seabeck	Willcox House	B-2
Seattle	B.D. Williams House	B-3
Seattle	Chambered Nautilus	B-3
Seattle	Salisbury House	B-3
Seattle	Soundview	B-3
Sequim	Glenna's Guthrie Cottage	B-2
Sequim	Granny Sandy's Orchard	B-2
Silverdale	Heaven's Edge	B-2
Tacoma	Chinaberry Hill	C-3
Tacoma	The Villa	C-3
Trout Lake	Llama Ranch	E-3
Vashon Island	Mimi's Cottage by the Sea	C-2
Wenatchee	Rimrock Inn	C-4
Yakima	A Touch of Europe	D-4

Breads & Muffins

Breads
&
Muffins

B.D. Williams House

The B.D. Williams House Bed and Breakfast is a turn-of-the-century house that sits atop historic Queen Anne Hill near downtown Seattle. Much of the original woodwork, gas light fixtures and lincrusta wall coverings have been retained.

"Slept like a baby. Could there really have been a full house of guests?"

~ Guest, B.D. Williams House

INNKEEPERS: *Susan & Doug Williams*
ADDRESS: *1505 4th Avenue North*
Seattle, WA 98109
TELEPHONE: *(206) 285-0810; (800) 880-0810*
FAX: *(206) 285-8526*
E-MAIL: *innkeepr@wolfenet.com*
WEBSITE: *Not Available*
ROOMS: *5 Rooms; All with private baths*
OPEN: *Year-round*
CHILDREN: *Children allowed (All by prior arrangement)*
ANIMALS: *Prohibited*
SMOKING: *Prohibited*

Zucchini Bread

Makes 2 loaves

This versatile batter can be baked into loaves of bread, or used to make cake-like frosted bars. Either way, the results are delicious!

4 eggs
2 cups sugar
1 cup vegetable oil
1 teaspoon vanilla
3 cups flour
1 teaspoon salt
1 teaspoon baking soda
2 teaspoons cinnamon
3 cups grated fresh zucchini (about 4 or 5 small zucchini)
1 1/2 cups coconut
1 1/2 cups chopped walnuts or pecans

PREHEAT OVEN TO 350°F. Grease and flour two 9x5-inch loaf pans. In a large bowl, beat together eggs, sugar, oil and vanilla. Sift in flour, salt, baking soda and cinnamon. Mix until smooth. Stir in zucchini, coconut and nuts. Pour batter into prepared pans. Bake for approximately 60 minutes, or until toothpick inserted in center of loaf comes out clean.

Frosted Zucchini Bars

Makes 40 (1 1/2 x 2 1/2-inch) bars

PREHEAT OVEN TO 350°F. Grease and flour a 10x15-inch jelly-roll pan. Mix ingredients according to the above recipe. Pour batter into prepared pan and bake for approximately 25-30 minutes. Test for doneness with a toothpick. When completely cooled, frost with Cream Cheese Frosting. Cut into bars. Keep refrigerated.

Cream Cheese Frosting

3 ounces cream cheese, room temperature
6 tablespoons butter, room temperature
1 tablespoon milk
1 teaspoon vanilla
3 cups powdered sugar

In a medium bowl, beat together cream cheese, butter, milk and vanilla. Add powdered sugar. Beat until smooth.

Ravenscroft

L ocated high on a bluff, the Ravenscroft Inn overlooks Port Townsend Bay, Admiralty Inlet and the Cascade Mountains. Originally built in 1987 as a replication of a historic Charleston Single House, guests enjoy spacious rooms, private fireplaces and verandahs.

The multi-course breakfast that includes fresh fruit, frappe, homemade muffins, coffeecake and a special entrée is a gourmet's delight.

INNKEEPERS: *Leah Hammer*
ADDRESS: *533 Quincy Street*
Port Townsend, WA 98368
TELEPHONE: *(360) 385-2784; (800) 782-2691*
FAX: *(360) 385-6724*
E-MAIL: *ravenscroft@olympus.net*
WEBSITE: *www.olympus.net/ravenscroft/*
ROOMS: *6 Rooms; 2 Suites; All with private baths*
OPEN: *Year-round*
CHILDREN: *Children 12 and older are welcome*
ANIMALS: *Prohibited*
SMOKING: *Prohibited*

Carrot-Zucchini Bread
à la Ravenscroft

Makes 2 loaves

3 eggs
1 3/4 cups sugar
1 cup vegetable oil
2 teaspoons vanilla
2 1/3 cups flour
2 teaspoons baking soda
1/4 teaspoon baking powder
1 teaspoon salt
1 teaspoon cinnamon
1 1/2 cups grated zucchini, drained (squeeze out moisture)
1 1/2 cups grated carrots
1 cup chopped nuts
1/2 cup raisins, chocolate chips or coconut (optional)

PREHEAT OVEN TO 350°F. Coat two 9x5-inch loaf pans with nonstick cooking spray. In a large bowl, combine eggs, sugar, oil and vanilla. Sift in flour, baking soda, baking powder, salt and cinnamon. Mix well. Stir in zucchini, carrots, nuts and any optional ingredients, if using. Divide batter evenly between the two prepared pans. Bake for approximately 60 minutes, or until a toothpick inserted in center of loaves comes out clean. Cool for about 10 minutes on a wire rack before removing loaves from pans.

Chambered Nautilus

T he Chambered Nautilus Bed and Breakfast, named for the beautiful Pacific seashell, was built in 1915 by Herbert and Annie Gowen. Dr. Gowen was among the early faculty at the University of Washington where he founded the department of Oriental Studies.

This elegant Georgian Colonial home is located on a peaceful hill just ten minutes from downtown Seattle and a short walk from the University of Washington campus.

INNKEEPERS:	*Joyce Schulte & Steven Poole*
ADDRESS:	*5005 22nd Avenue NE*
	Seattle, WA 98105
TELEPHONE:	*(206) 522-2536; (800) 545-8459*
FAX:	*(206) 528-0898*
E-MAIL:	*chamberednautilus@msn.com*
WEBSITE:	*www.virtualcities.com*
ROOMS:	*6 Rooms; All with private baths*
OPEN:	*Year-round*
CHILDREN:	*Children over the age of 8 are welcome with prior arrangement*
ANIMALS:	*Prohibited*
SMOKING:	*Prohibited*

Cranberry-Orange Bread

Makes 1 loaf

2 tablespoons butter or margarine, room temperature
1 egg
1 cup sugar
3/4 cup orange juice
1/4 teaspoon orange extract
2 cups flour
1 teaspoon baking powder
1/2 teaspoon baking soda
1/2 teaspoon salt
2 cups whole fresh or frozen cranberries (if frozen, thaw before
    using)
1/2 cup chopped walnuts

PREHEAT OVEN TO 350°F. Grease a 9x5-inch loaf pan. In a large bowl, combine butter or margarine, egg and sugar. Mix well. Add orange juice and orange extract. Sift in flour, baking powder, baking soda and salt. Stir until just moistened. Fold in cranberries and nuts. Spoon batter into loaf pan. Bake for approximately 60 minutes, or until a toothpick inserted in center of the loaf comes out clean. Cool on wire rack for 10-20 minutes before removing loaf from pan.

"This is a great year-round treat. Buy the cranberries fresh when in season and freeze to use later. Traditionally a holiday treat, guests love to be surprised with warm cranberry bread on the breakfast table in the middle of summer!"

Joyce Schulte - Chambered Nautilus

Duffy House

H ospitality is an art at the Duffy House Bed and Breakfast Inn. Located near Friday Harbor, it commands a splendid view of Griffin Bay and the snow-capped Olympic Mountains.

This fully-restored, 1920's Tudor-style home exudes warmth and comfort for its guests. A mooring buoy is available off the beach in front of the house.

INNKEEPERS:	*Mary & Arthur Miller*
ADDRESS:	*760 Pear Point Road*
	Friday Harbor, WA 98250
TELEPHONE:	*(360) 378-5604; (800) 972-2089*
FAX:	*(360) 378-6535*
E-MAIL:	*duffyhouse@rockisland.com*
WEBSITE:	*www.pacificrim.net/~bydesign/duffy.html*
ROOMS:	*5 Rooms; All with private baths*
OPEN:	*Year-round*
CHILDREN:	*Children over the age of 8 are welcome with prior arrangement*
ANIMALS:	*Prohibited*
SMOKING:	*Permitted outside only*

Prune Bread

Makes 2 loaves

3 eggs
2 cups sugar
1 cup vegetable oil
1 cup buttermilk
1 cup cooked prunes, drained and puréed (see below)
2 1/4 cups flour
1 teaspoon baking soda
1 teaspoon cinnamon
1 teaspoon nutmeg
1 teaspoon allspice
1 cup chopped nuts
Whipped cream, cream cheese or lemon curd (optional)

PREHEAT OVEN TO 350°F. Grease and flour two 9x5-inch loaf pans. In a large bowl, combine eggs, sugar, oil, buttermilk and prune purée. Sift together flour, baking soda, cinnamon, nutmeg and allspice. Toss nuts in flour/spice mixture to coat nuts. Stir all ingredients together until just moistened. Spoon batter into prepared loaf pans. Bake for approximately 60 minutes, or until a toothpick inserted in center of loaves comes out clean. Let cool on a wire rack for 10-20 minutes before removing bread from pans. Let set for awhile, then slice and serve warm. Whipped cream, softened cream cheese or lemon curd make nice accompaniments.

To cook prunes: In a small saucepan, cover the dried fruit with water. Simmer approximately 15 minutes.

To purée prunes: Whirl the drained prunes in a blender or food processor.

Home by the Sea

Overlooking a wildlife sanctuary, Home by the Sea Bed and Breakfast is located on picturesque Whidbey Island. The Sandpiper Suite offers a private garden entrance, kitchen, dining and living room areas, woodburning stove, outdoor Jacuzzi and a private deck.

Home by the Sea was the first bed and breakfast on Whidbey Island.

INNKEEPERS:	*Sharon Fritts Drew, Helen Launtz Fritts & Linda Drew Walsh*
ADDRESS:	*2388 East Sunlight Beach Road Clinton, WA 98236*
TELEPHONE:	*(360) 321-2964*
FAX:	*(360) 321-4378*
E-MAIL:	*Not Available*
WEBSITE:	*www.frenchroadfarm.com*
ROOMS:	*1 Suite; 2 Cottages; All with private baths*
OPEN:	*Year-round*
CHILDREN:	*Children welcome*
ANIMALS:	*Welcome (Cats and dogs permitted in 1 suite and 1 cottage)*
SMOKING:	*Prohibited*

Jenny's Norwegian Brown Bread

Makes 3 loaves (or 9 small loaves)

3 1/2 cups sugar
4 cups water
1 (15-ounce) box raisins
2 cups cold water
3/4 cup shortening
2 tablespoons baking soda
1 teaspoon salt
2 teaspoons ground cloves
1 teaspoon cinnamon, or more to taste
7 cups flour
1 cup chopped nuts
Maraschino cherries or candied mixed fruit (optional)

PREHEAT OVEN TO 375°F. Grease three 9x5-inch loaf pans or nine 5x3-inch pans. In a very large saucepan or stockpot, mix sugar and 4 cups of water. Add raisins and bring to a boil. Simmer about 10 minutes to plump raisins. Remove from heat. Stir in two cups cold water, shortening, baking soda, salt, cloves and cinnamon. Mix well. Add flour and mix until all ingredients are thoroughly combined. Add nuts. Pour batter into prepared loaf pans. (If desired, top with maraschino cherries or candied mixed fruit at Christmas.) Bake regular size loaves for approximately 60 minutes or small loaves for approximately 25 minutes.

"My grandmother Jenny brought this recipe (in her head) from Norway in 1914. When I asked her for the recipe, she said, 'A pan of water, a sifter of flour, etc.' I had to measure out this final recipe. This bread slices nicely for Christmas plates with doilies. Or wrap it in plastic wrap with ribbon and a bow for gift giving. Five generations of our family now bake this bread."

Sharon Fritts Drew - Home by the Sea

Holly Hedge House

B lending coziness and charm, the Holly Hedge House Bed and Breakfast offers an unassuming elegance of a bygone era. Located less than ten minutes from SeaTac Airport and fifteen minutes from the downtown Seattle area, this unique getaway is within walking distance of restaurants, antique shops and outdoor water sports.

Guests enjoy jogging and biking trails along the picturesque Cedar River.

INNKEEPERS: *Lynn & Marian Thrasher*
ADDRESS: *908 Grant Avenue South*
Renton, WA 98055
TELEPHONE: *(425) 226-2555; (888) 226-2555*
FAX: *(425) 226-2555*
E-MAIL: *holihedg@nwlink.com*
WEBSITE: *www.nwlink.com/~holihedg*
ROOMS: *1 Cottage; Private bath*
OPEN: *Year-round*
CHILDREN: *Prohibited*
ANIMALS: *Prohibited*
SMOKING: *Prohibited*

Banana Oatmeal Chocolate Chip Muffins

Makes 12 muffins

A delicious and creative way to use leftover cooked oatmeal! These muffins are very moist.

1/2 cup shortening
1 cup sugar
1 egg
1 teaspoon vanilla
2 ripe bananas, mashed
1 cup cooked oatmeal
2 cups flour
1 teaspoon baking soda
1/2 teaspoon salt
1/2 cup mini chocolate chips

PREHEAT OVEN TO 350°F. Grease 12 muffin cups. In a large bowl, cream together shortening, sugar, egg and vanilla. Add mashed bananas and cooked oatmeal. Sift in flour, baking soda and salt. Stir just until dry ingredients are moistened. Stir in chocolate chips. Spoon batter into prepared muffin cups. Bake for 22-25 minutes, or until done. Cool on a wire rack for 10-15 minutes, then remove muffins from pans. Good served warm or cold.

Quimper Inn

Originally built by Henry Morgan in 1888 as a simple, two-bedroom home, the Quimper Inn was refurbished in 1904 by Harry and Gertrud Barthrop. Harry and Gertie's Suite, named after the Barthrops, features breathtaking views of the Olympic Mountains, Port Townsend Bay, Admiralty Inlet and Jefferson County's 100-year-old clock tower.

This grand home is located within walking distance of historic Port Townsend.

INNKEEPERS:	*Sue & Ron Ramage*
ADDRESS:	*1306 Franklin Street*
	Port Townsend, WA 98368
TELEPHONE:	*(360) 385-1060; (800) 557-1060*
FAX:	*(360) 385-2688*
E-MAIL:	*thequimps@olympus.net*
WEBSITE:	*www.olympus.net/biz/quimper/quimper.html*
ROOMS:	*5 Rooms; 1 Suite; Private and shared baths*
OPEN:	*Year-round*
CHILDREN:	*Children over the age of 12 are welcome*
ANIMALS:	*Prohibited*
SMOKING:	*Prohibited indoors; Permitted outside yard*

Banana Blueberry Muffins

Makes 12 muffins

To vary this recipe, in the fall try substituting cranberries for the blueberries and add 1/2 cup of chopped walnuts.

2 large, ripe bananas
1/2 cup nonfat banana yogurt
1 egg, beaten
1 1/2 cups flour
3/4 cup sugar
1 1/2 teaspoons baking soda
1 cup blueberries, fresh or frozen

PREHEAT OVEN TO 350°F. Grease 12 muffin cups. In a large bowl, mash the bananas. Add yogurt and egg; mix completely. Add the flour, sugar and baking soda; stir just until dry ingredients are moistened. Gently fold in blueberries. Spoon batter into prepared muffin cups, about 3/4 full. Bake for approximately 30 minutes, or until tops of muffins are golden brown. Cool on a wire rack for 10 minutes before removing muffins from pan.

"I devised this muffin recipe for the growing number of guests who request low-fat foods."

Sue Ramage - Quimper Inn

Carol's Corner

I used fat-free banana crème pie flavored yogurt to test this recipe and the muffins were great! If you are using frozen blueberries and they are icy, quickly rinse them with cold water and pat dry with paper towels. Do this just before adding them to the batter. Do not let them thaw. This step helps prevent discoloring the muffin batter.

Spring Bay Inn

Spring Bay Inn on Orcas Island is a secluded retreat that rests quietly on its own spectacular water frontage. Over 250 custom windows tempt guests to stay inside to enjoy views of the water and forest.

High ceilings, Rumford fireplaces and walls lined with musical instruments provide a feeling of informal elegance.

INNKEEPERS:	*Carl Burger & Sandy Playa*
ADDRESS:	*Obstruction Pass Trailhead Road*
	Olga, Orcas Island WA 98279
TELEPHONE:	*(360) 376-5531*
FAX:	*(360) 376-2193*
E-MAIL:	*kayakinn@rockisland.com*
WEBSITE:	*www.springbayinn.com*
ROOMS:	*5 Rooms; All with private baths*
OPEN:	*Year-round*
CHILDREN:	*Welcome (Must be over 10 to kayak)*
ANIMALS:	*Prohibited*
SMOKING:	*Prohibited*

Ginger Apple Muffins

Makes 7 dozen muffins

These are wonderful served straight from the oven!

4 cups milk
2 2/3 cups butter, melted and cooled
8 eggs, lightly beaten
8 teaspoons vanilla
14 cups flour
4 cups sugar
7 tablespoons baking powder
2 teaspoons salt
2 teaspoons ground nutmeg
6 teaspoons ground ginger
8 apples, peeled and diced

PREHEAT OVEN TO 400°F. Grease muffin cups or use paper liners. In a very large bowl, combine milk, melted butter, eggs and vanilla. Combine dry ingredients and mix with apples. Add dry ingredients to wet ingredients and blend together, using as few strokes as possible. Spoon batter into prepared muffin pans, about 2/3 full. Bake for 15-20 minutes.

Carol's Corner

Leftover batter can be stored in the refrigerator overnight and baked the next day. Bring batter to room temperature (do not stir) and spoon into muffin cups. You can also easily make just 1/4 of this large recipe. Use the following quantities:
1 cup milk, 2/3 cup butter, 2 eggs, 2 teaspoons vanilla, 3 1/2 cups flour, 1 cup sugar,
1 3/4 tablespoons baking powder, 1/2 teaspoon salt,
1/2 teaspoon nutmeg, 1 1/2 teaspoons ginger and
2 apples. Makes 21 muffins.

Caswell's on the Bay

Situated on three and one-half secluded acres at the edge of Willapa Bay, Caswell's on the Bay Bed and Breakfast Inn offers the ambiance of yesteryear. The five spacious antique-appointed rooms feature queen-sized beds and private sitting areas.

"Staying here was like checking into heaven."

~ Guest, Caswell's on the Bay

INNKEEPERS:	*Bob & Marilyn Caswell*
ADDRESS:	*25204 Sandridge Road*
	Ocean Park, WA 98640
TELEPHONE:	*(360) 665-6535*
FAX:	*(360) 665-6500*
E-MAIL:	*Not Available*
WEBSITE:	*www.site-works.com/caswells*
ROOMS:	*5 Rooms; All with private baths*
OPEN:	*Year-round*
CHILDREN:	*Children over the age of 12 are welcome*
ANIMALS:	*Prohibited*
SMOKING:	*Permitted outdoors only*

Sour Cream Apple-Cranberry Muffins

Makes 18 muffins (or 12 giant size)

2 cups unbleached, all-purpose flour
3/4 cup sugar
1 tablespoon baking powder
3/4 teaspoon baking soda
1 teaspoon ground cinnamon
1/4 teaspoon ground nutmeg
1/4 teaspoon ground allspice
1/4 teaspoon ground cloves
1/4 teaspoon salt
1 cup dried cranberries
2 eggs, beaten
4 tablespoons butter, melted
1 1/2 cups low-fat or nonfat sour cream
1 cup chopped Granny Smith apples
Topping (recipe to follow)

PREHEAT OVEN TO 375°F. Coat muffin pans with nonstick cooking spray. In a large bowl, combine first 10 ingredients (flour through dried cranberries). Set aside. In a small bowl, combine eggs, melted butter, sour cream and apples. Make a large well in dry ingredients. Pour liquid ingredients (eggs through apples) into well. Mix just until blended. Fill muffin cups 2/3 full with batter. Sprinkle about 1 teaspoon topping over each muffin. Bake for approximately 15-20 minutes, or until lightly browned. Test for doneness with a toothpick. Do not overbake. Let cool about 5 minutes before removing muffins from pans.

Topping

1/2 cup brown sugar
1/3 cup flour
4 tablespoons cold, firm butter

In a small bowl, mix together brown sugar and flour. Cut in butter until ingredients are crumbly. This recipe will make enough for 3 to 4 batches. Cover tightly any remaining topping and store in refrigerator for up to 3 weeks.

Growly Bear

Originally built in 1890, the Growly Bear Bed and Breakfast is a rustic homestead with captivating mountain views. Located five miles east of Ashford and one mile from the Nisqually entrance to Mount Rainier National Park, this secluded home provides a spectacular setting for a private getaway.

Guests awaken to the tantalizing aroma of freshly baked bread.

INNKEEPERS:	*Susan Jenny Johnson*
ADDRESS:	*37311 SR 706*
	Ashford, WA 98304
TELEPHONE:	*(360) 569-2339*
FAX:	*Not Available*
E-MAIL:	*Not Available*
WEBSITE:	*Not Available*
ROOMS:	*2 Rooms; 1 Suite; Private and shared baths*
OPEN:	*Year-round*
CHILDREN:	*Welcome*
ANIMALS:	*Prohibited*
SMOKING:	*Prohibited*

Huckleberry-Sunflower Muffins

Makes 3 dozen muffins

1 cup margarine, melted and cooled
6 eggs
1 cup milk
3 cups flour
1 1/2 cups sugar
4 teaspoons baking powder
1/2 teaspoon salt
1 cup unprocessed bran
1 1/2 cups sunflower seeds, raw or roasted
3 cups huckleberries (or blueberries)

PREHEAT OVEN TO 375°F. Grease muffin pans. In a large bowl, beat together melted margarine, eggs and milk. Set aside. In another large bowl, combine flour, sugar, baking powder, salt and bran. Add sunflower seeds and huckleberries; toss to combine with dry ingredients. Stir dry ingredients into milk mixture just until moistened. Fill muffin cups 2/3 full. Bake for approximately 20 minutes, or until done.

Carol's Corner

A huckleberry is very similar in appearance and taste to a blueberry. They are not cultivated, however, so if you want fresh huckleberries you'll have to pick them yourself or purchase from a farmers' market. They are excellent in muffins, pies and other baked goods.

Chambered Nautilus

Perched on a peaceful hill in Seattle's University district, the Chambered Nautilus Bed and Breakfast Inn is an elegant 1915 Georgian Colonial home. Located ten minutes from downtown Seattle, this lovely inn offers large guest rooms, attractive gardens and views of the Cascade Mountains.

Amenities include fresh flowers, bottled water, soft robes and a resident teddy bear.

INNKEEPERS:	*Joyce Schulte & Steven Poole*
ADDRESS:	*5005 22nd Avenue NE*
	Seattle, WA 98105
TELEPHONE:	*(206) 522-2536; (800) 545-8459*
FAX:	*(206) 528-0898*
E-MAIL:	*chamberednautilus@msn.com*
WEBSITE:	*www.virtualcities.com*
ROOMS:	*6 Rooms; All with private baths*
OPEN:	*Year-round*
CHILDREN:	*Children over the age of 8 are welcome with prior arrangement only*
ANIMALS:	*Prohibited*
SMOKING:	*Prohibited*

Rosemary Buttermilk Muffins

Makes 12 muffins

2 cups unbleached, all-purpose flour
2 tablespoons sugar
4 teaspoons baking powder
1/2 teaspoon baking soda
1/2 teaspoon salt
1/2 teaspoon onion powder
1 teaspoon dried rosemary, crushed
1/2 cup shortening, melted
1 cup buttermilk
2 tablespoons grated Parmesan cheese

Position rack in center of oven. PREHEAT OVEN TO 400°F. Grease muffin cups. In a large bowl, sift together flour, sugar, baking powder, baking soda, salt and onion powder. Stir in crushed rosemary. Make a well in center of dry ingredients; set aside. In a medium bowl, whisk melted shortening with buttermilk; beat thoroughly. Pour into well of dry ingredients, stirring only until flour is moistened. Spoon batter into muffin cups. Sprinkle tops with Parmesan cheese. Bake for 15 minutes, or until golden brown. Cool slightly for 5 minutes in pan before turning onto wire rack. Serve warm.

Carol's Corner

For a light texture, <u>gently</u> spoon the dough into the muffin cups; avoid pressing the dough down. These are delicious, savory muffins!

Biscuits, Rolls, Coffee Cake & Scones

Biscuits
Rolls
Coffee Cake
&
Scones

Tudor Inn

O riginally built in 1910, the Tudor Inn Bed and Breakfast has been tastefully restored to retain the rustic charm of the Tudor era and modernized to provide the comfort and ease of the present. The inn has many fine antiques that are on sale in the library.

The first owner was a dentist from England. After seasoning a piece of wood, he took it to the third floor where he built a coffin in which he was later buried.

INNKEEPERS:	*Jane Glass*
ADDRESS:	*1108 South Oak Street*
	Port Angeles, WA 98362
TELEPHONE:	*(360) 452-3138*
FAX:	*Not Available*
E-MAIL:	*tudorinfo@aol.com*
WEBSITE:	*www.northolympic.com/tudorinn*
ROOMS:	*5 Rooms; All with private baths*
OPEN:	*Year-round*
CHILDREN:	*Children over the age of 12 are welcome*
ANIMALS:	*Prohibited*
SMOKING:	*Permitted on porch*

Angel Biscuits

Makes approximately 24 biscuits

1 package active dry yeast
2 tablespoons warm water
5 cups flour
1 teaspoon baking soda
3 teaspoons baking powder
1 teaspoon salt
2 tablespoons sugar
1 cup butter, room temperature, + additional butter (melted) for
brushing tops of biscuits before baking
2 cups buttermilk

PREHEAT OVEN TO 400°F. In a small bowl, dissolve yeast in warm water. Set aside. In a large bowl, sift together dry ingredients. Cut in softened (not melted) butter with pastry blender. Add buttermilk and yeast mixture. Stir until thoroughly moistened. Turn out onto floured board; knead for a minute or two. Roll out to desired thickness and cut into rounds. (If rolled 3/4-inch thick, and cut with a 2 1/2-inch cutter, yield will be about 24 biscuits.) Brush with melted butter. Bake on an ungreased cookie sheet for 12-15 minutes.

White Rose Inn

O riginally built in 1922 by Axel G. Hanson, owner of the White River Lumber Company, the White Rose Inn is a 22-room colonial mansion that was constructed with beautiful Honduran mahogany, quarter sawn oak and other elegant accents.

The refined and spacious first floor reception room features a coved ceiling and is perfect for weddings, meetings, banquets and other special functions.

INNKEEPERS:	*Reggie & John Ulness*
ADDRESS:	*1610 Griffin Avenue*
	Enumclaw, WA 98022
TELEPHONE:	*(360) 825-7194; (800) 404-7194*
FAX:	*Not Available*
E-MAIL:	*whiterose@firstdial.com*
WEBSITE:	*www.firstdial.com/~whiterose*
ROOMS:	*4 Rooms; All with private baths*
OPEN:	*Year-round*
CHILDREN:	*Welcome*
ANIMALS:	*Prohibited*
SMOKING:	*Prohibited*

Apricot Pillows

Makes 10 biscuits

These biscuits are fun to serve with scrambled eggs and bacon. To save time, prepared fillings such as jam, preserves or apple butter can be substituted for the apricot filling. Use several different flavors of jam to give your guests a choice!

Filling

2 cups cleaned, seeded and chopped fresh apricots
1/3 cup sugar
2 tablespoons water

Biscuits

2 cups flour
1/4 cup sugar
2 teaspoons baking powder
1/4 teaspoon cinnamon (may use up to 1/2 teaspoon)
1/2 cup (1 stick) butter or margarine, chilled
1 egg
1/4 cup milk

Glaze

1 egg, lightly beaten

Topping

2 tablespoons sugar

PREHEAT OVEN TO 400°F. Line a baking sheet with foil; grease foil. To prepare filling: In a small saucepan, combine apricots, sugar and water. Simmer over medium heat until thickened, about 15 minutes.

To prepare biscuits: In a large bowl, sift together flour, sugar, baking powder and cinnamon. Using a pastry blender, cut butter into flour mixture until coarse crumbs form. In a small bowl, mix together egg and milk. Add to flour mixture and stir until dough forms. If dough is too dry, a bit more milk may be added. Divide dough in half. On a lightly floured surface, roll first half of dough into a 10x8-inch rectangle. Cut into 5 strips each measuring 2x8-inches. Spread one tablespoon apricot filling or jam down center of each strip to within 1/2-inch of all edges. Fold dough in half to form a "pillow". Pinch edges together (press with fork tines for a decorative edge). Repeat with other half of dough. Brush pillow tops with egg glaze and sprinkle with sugar. Bake biscuits until golden, about 12-15 minutes. Transfer to wire rack. Serve warm. Biscuits are also excellent cold as a snack.

Blue Heron Inn

Sitting at the edge of Silver Lake, the Blue Heron Inn Bed and Breakfast offers a panoramic view of Mount St. Helens and its forested valleys. Located on five acres, this beautiful getaway is perfect for private parties, business meetings and weddings.

Guests relax in the spacious parlor, browse through a fine book selection in the library or relax on the covered verandah.

INNKEEPERS:	*John & Jeanne Robards*
ADDRESS:	*2846 Spirit Lake Highway*
	Castle Rock, WA 98611
TELEPHONE:	*(360) 274-9595; (800) 959-4049*
FAX:	*Not Available*
E-MAIL:	*jeanne@blueheroninn.com*
WEBSITE:	*www.blueheroninn.com*
ROOMS:	*6 Rooms; All with private baths*
OPEN:	*Year-round*
CHILDREN:	*Children over the age of 6 are welcome*
ANIMALS:	*Prohibited*
SMOKING:	*Permitted on outside decks and patios*

Bubble Bread

Makes 8-12 servings

Easy and spectacular! A winner!

1/2 cup chopped nuts
24 frozen dough dinner rolls
1 cup brown sugar
1 (3.5-ounce) package butterscotch pudding and pie filling dry mix
  (do not use instant)
1/4 cup sugar
1 teaspoon cinnamon
3/4 cup (1 1/2 sticks) butter, melted

Grease and flour (or coat with nonstick cooking spray) a 10-inch Bundt pan. Sprinkle nuts into bottom of pan. Place frozen dinner rolls over nuts; distribute evenly. In a small bowl, mix together brown sugar, pudding mix, sugar and cinnamon. Sprinkle this mixture over rolls. Pour melted butter over the mixture and rolls. Leave pan uncovered on countertop overnight.

Note: You may want to place a cookie sheet under the Bundt pan just in case the rolls spill over a bit during the rising process. This is more likely to happen if your kitchen is very warm.

Next morning: PREHEAT OVEN TO 350°F. and bake for 30 minutes. Cool for 2 minutes. Invert pan onto a rimmed platter, as topping will run.

Nantucket Manor

L ocated on the Squamish Harbor of the Hood Canal, the Nantucket Manor Bed and Breakfast affords panoramic views of Mount Rainier, the Cascade Range and the Olympic Mountains. This exquisite beachside retreat features museum quality art, European and American antiques and a garden gazebo.

Guests enjoy whale watching while strolling on the private sandy beach.

INNKEEPERS:	*Peter & Peggy Conrardy*
ADDRESS:	*941 Shine Road*
	Port Ludlow, WA 98365
TELEPHONE:	*(360) 437-2676*
FAX:	*(360) 437-2791*
E-MAIL:	*Not Available*
WEBSITE:	*www.olympus.net/biz/nantucket/*
ROOMS:	*5 Rooms; All with private baths*
OPEN:	*Year-round*
CHILDREN:	*Children over the age of 12 are welcome*
ANIMALS:	*Prohibited*
SMOKING:	*Permitted on outside verandah, balconies and terrace*

Cinnamon Pecan Rolls

Makes 15-18 rolls

3 1/2 to 4 1/2 cups bread flour, divided
3 tablespoons sugar
1 teaspoon salt
1 1/2 tablespoons active dry yeast
1 cup milk
1/2 cup water
1/4 cup butter

<u>Topping</u>

1/2 cup butter, melted
1/2 cup light brown sugar
1/2 cup chopped pecans

<u>Filling</u>

2 tablespoons butter, room temperature
1/2 cup light brown sugar
1 tablespoon cinnamon
Optional: 1/3 cup raisins soaked in 1 tablespoon brown sugar and
    2 tablespoons hot water, drained

In a large bowl, combine 1 1/2 cups of the flour, sugar, salt and yeast. In a microwave-safe cup, combine milk, water and butter; heat in microwave until warm. Add milk mixture to dry ingredients and mix 1-2 minutes until ingredients are well combined. Gradually add the additional flour until dough "licks" bowl clean of flour, but is still slightly tacky. Knead dough on floured board until elastic, about 5-10 minutes. Place dough in an oiled bowl, turning dough to coat with oil. Cover with towel; place in dishwasher that has been placed on dry cycle to desired warmth. Also add a pan of hot water in dishwasher for humidity; allow dough to proof until size doubles, about 15 minutes. <u>While dough is rising, prepare topping</u>: Pour melted butter in a 13x9-inch pan. Add brown sugar to melted butter; mix with fork, spreading evenly over bottom of pan. Sprinkle with pecans. Place risen dough on floured board; roll into a 10x18-inch rectangle. <u>To make filling</u>: Spread the 2 tablespoons butter on the dough. In a small bowl, mix together brown sugar and cinnamon. Sprinkle mixture on top of buttered dough. Sprinkle with drained raisins, if desired. Roll dough lengthwise; cut into 15 or 18 slices. Place slices evenly in 3 rows of 5 or 6 rolls each. (<u>Make-ahead tip</u>: The rolls may be covered and refrigerated at this point until morning.)

<u>When ready to bake</u>: PREHEAT OVEN TO 375°F. Proof rolls in dishwasher as described above, then bake uncovered for 25 minutes. Cool for 2-5 minutes. Invert pan onto serving plate.

Rimrock Inn

Named for the rocks that rim the top of Pitcher Canyon, Rimrock Inn Bed and Breakfast is located between Wenatchee and the Mission Ridge ski area.

For a weekend each May, Wenatchee celebrates its heritage in the fruit industry with the Washington State Apple Blossom Festival. Activities include the Grand and Kiddies parade, art and food in the park and carnival rides.

INNKEEPERS:	*Doug & Mary Cook*
ADDRESS:	*1354 Pitcher Canyon Road*
	Wenatchee, WA 98801
TELEPHONE:	*(509) 664-5113; (888) 664-5113*
FAX:	*(509) 664-5113*
E-MAIL:	*Not Available*
WEBSITE:	*www.cascadeloop.com/option3/rimrock*
ROOMS:	*3 Rooms; All with private baths*
OPEN:	*Year-round*
CHILDREN:	*Children 10 and older are welcome*
ANIMALS:	*Prohibited*
SMOKING:	*Prohibited*

Sour Cream Orange Rolls

Makes 8 rolls

1 package active dry yeast
1/2 cup warm water
1/4 cup (1/2 stick) butter, room temperature
2 eggs
1/2 cup sour cream
3 1/2 cups flour
1 teaspoon salt
2 tablespoons sugar

Filling

1/4 cup (1/2 stick) butter, room temperature
3/4 cup sugar
2 tablespoons grated orange peel (zest)

In a large bowl, dissolve yeast in warm water. Add butter, eggs, sour cream, flour, salt and sugar; mix well. Place dough on well-floured board; knead for 5-8 minutes. (Keep hands and board well floured during the kneading process.) Place dough in an oiled bowl, turning dough to coat with oil. Cover with clean towel or plastic wrap; let rise until doubled in size. For the filling, in a small bowl, combine sugar and orange peel. Set aside. Roll dough into a 10x12-inch rectangle. Spread butter over dough. Sprinkle sugar/orange peel mixture over buttered dough. Starting with 12-inch side, roll dough jelly-roll fashion; pinch seam to seal. Cut into 8 rolls (each about 1 1/2-inches thick). Arrange rolls, cut-side down, in a greased 11x7-inch pan. Cover loosely, and let rise for 40-45 minutes. PREHEAT OVEN TO 350°F. Bake rolls for 25 minutes, or until golden. Cool slightly. While rolls are still in pan and warm, glaze tops of rolls with Orange Icing.

Orange Icing

1/2 cup sugar
1/4 cup sour cream
1/4 cup butter
3 tablespoons orange juice

In a medium saucepan, combine all ingredients. Boil for 3 minutes, stirring occasionally. Cool slightly, then glaze tops of rolls while icing and rolls are both still warm.

The Pillars

S ituated on two acres of landscaped and wooded grounds, The Pillars
Bed and Breakfast overlooks Puget Sound, with views of Colvos
Passage, Vashon Island and Mount Rainier.

The dining room's eastern exposure to the water and the mountains offers
a fitting scenic complement to a delectable breakfast that includes
home-baked breads and muffins, fresh seasonal fruit and natural cereals.

INNKEEPERS:	*Alma & Jim Boge*
ADDRESS:	*6606 Soundview Drive*
	Gig Harbor, WA 98335
TELEPHONE:	*(253) 851-6644*
FAX:	*Not Available*
E-MAIL:	*Not Available*
WEBSITE:	*Not Available*
ROOMS:	*3 Rooms; All with private baths*
OPEN:	*April through October*
CHILDREN:	*Children over the age of 10 are welcome*
ANIMALS:	*Prohibited*
SMOKING:	*Prohibited*

Cinnamon Streusel
Buttermilk Coffee Cake

Makes 8 servings

Buttermilk Coffee Cake

1 cup buttermilk
1/4 cup vegetable oil
1 tablespoon orange extract
1/3 cup sugar
1 3/4 cups baking mix (such as Bisquick)

Cinnamon Streusel Topping

1/3 cup margarine, room temperature
2/3 cup sugar
1 tablespoon cinnamon (more or less to taste)
2/3 cup flour
Chunky applesauce and/or vanilla yogurt (optional toppings)

Place rack in upper middle of oven. PREHEAT OVEN TO 375°F. Thoroughly coat sides and bottom of 10x7-inch baking pan with nonstick cooking spray. In a large bowl, mix together all coffee cake ingredients, scraping sides and bottom of bowl with rubber scraper. Pour batter evenly into pan; be sure all corners are filled.

To prepare streusel topping: In a medium bowl, combine margarine, sugar and cinnamon until smooth. Stir in flour with a fork until uniformly crumbly. Sprinkle streusel topping evenly on top of coffee cake batter, reserving about 2 tablespoons. Using rubber scraper, randomly push some of the streusel topping into batter. Top with reserved streusel. Bake for 30 minutes. Remove from oven and allow to cool 10 minutes before cutting into pieces. Serve topped with warm, chunky applesauce (yummy!), or a dollop of vanilla yogurt, or both.

The Villa

THE VILLA

F rom its elegant, formal entrance to its beautiful gardens, The Villa Bed and Breakfast captures the charm of an Italian palazzo. With more than 7,000 square feet of space, it possesses a grand elegance.

Every room is full of serendipitous architectural spaces, artfully arranged in cozy nooks and light-filled spaces. A gourmet breakfast of seasonal delights is served each morning.

INNKEEPERS:	*Greg & Becky Anglemyer*
ADDRESS:	*705 North 5th Street*
	Tacoma, WA 98403
TELEPHONE:	*(253) 572-1157; (888) 572-1157*
FAX:	*(253) 572-1805*
E-MAIL:	*villabb@aol.com*
WEBSITE:	*www.tribnet.com/adv/bb/villa*
ROOMS:	*2 Rooms; 2 Suites; All with private baths*
OPEN:	*Year-round*
CHILDREN:	*Children 12 and older are welcome*
ANIMALS:	*Prohibited*
SMOKING:	*Prohibited*

Yogurt Coconut Coffee Cake

Makes 12 servings

A very moist, flavorful coffee cake! Perfect for your next brunch!

1/2 cup butter, room temperature
1/2 cup shortening
1 cup sugar
2 eggs
2 cups flour
1 teaspoon baking soda
1/2 teaspoon salt
1 cup vanilla or plain yogurt
1 teaspoon vanilla

Topping

1/3 cup sugar
1/3 cup brown sugar
1 teaspoon cinnamon
1/2 cup coconut

PREHEAT OVEN TO 350°F. Grease 13x9-inch baking dish. In a large bowl, cream butter, shortening and sugar. Beat in eggs. In a medium bowl, sift together flour, baking soda and salt. Add to butter mixture. Stir in yogurt and vanilla. Mix well. In a small bowl, combine topping ingredients; set aside. Drop half of batter by spoonfuls over the bottom of baking dish. (Batter is thick, so will have to be spread.) Sprinkle with half of topping. Spoon remaining batter in baking dish and spread carefully. Sprinkle with remaining topping. Bake for 30 minutes, or until toothpick inserted in center comes out clean. Watch carefully so the topping does not burn. Cool on wire rack

Make-ahead tip: This coffee cake can be baked a day in advance. It also freezes well.

Abendblume Pension

I nspired by the ambiance of fine European country inns, the Abendblume Pension Bed and Breakfast reflects this mood through its carved wood walls, archways, ceilings, deep inset windows and circular stairway.

Guest amenities include Alpine therapeutic massages for two, an outdoor spa, European bedding and luxurious baths with heated tile floors.

INNKEEPERS:	*Randy & Renee Sexauer*
ADDRESS:	*12570 Ranger Road*
	Leavenworth, WA 98826
TELEPHONE:	*(509) 548-4059; (800) 669-7634*
FAX:	*(509) 548-9032*
E-MAIL:	*abendblm@rightathome.com*
WEBSITE:	*www.abendblume.com*
ROOMS:	*7 Rooms; 4 Suites; All with private baths*
OPEN:	*Year-round*
CHILDREN:	*Prohibited*
ANIMALS:	*Prohibited*
SMOKING:	*Prohibited*

Blueberry Sour Cream Coffee Cake

Makes 12 servings

2 1/4 cups flour
2 teaspoons baking powder
1/2 teaspoon baking soda
1/2 teaspoon salt
3/4 cup butter, room temperature
3/4 cup sugar
1 teaspoon vanilla
2 eggs
1 cup sour cream
1 cup fresh or frozen blueberries (more or less)

Streusel Mixture

1/3 cup flour
1 teaspoon cinnamon
2/3 cup light brown sugar
1/4 cup (1/2 stick) cold, firm butter
2/3 cup chopped walnuts (may use up to 1 cup)

PREHEAT OVEN TO 350°F. Grease and flour 13x9-inch glass baking dish. In a medium bowl, sift together flour, baking powder, baking soda and salt. Set aside. In a large bowl, cream together butter, sugar and vanilla. Beat in eggs one at a time until fluffy. Add flour mixture to creamed butter/egg mixture alternately with sour cream.

To make streusel mixture: In a small bowl, combine flour, cinnamon and brown sugar. Using a pastry blender, cut in butter until mixture is crumbly. Stir in walnuts and set aside. Spread 1/2 batter into baking dish. Sprinkle with blueberries and 1/2 streusel mixture. Carefully spoon on remaining batter. Sprinkle with remaining streusel. Bake for approximately 40 minutes, or until a toothpick inserted in center of coffee cake comes out clean.

Lietz's

L ietz's Bed and Breakfast is a cozy country inn located four and one-half miles east of Leavenworth on the Wenatchee River. Guests savor the delicious, family-style breakfast that is served each morning from seven to ten o'clock.

Due to the close proximity of the Wenatchee River, guests can experience venturesome innertube float trips, the innertubes being provided by the inn.

INNKEEPERS:	*Verne & Helen Lietz*
ADDRESS:	*8305 Lynn Street*
	Peshastin, WA 98847
TELEPHONE:	*(509) 548-7504*
FAX:	*Not Available*
E-MAIL:	*Not Available*
WEBSITE:	*Not Available*
ROOMS:	*3 Rooms; Shared baths*
OPEN:	*Year-round*
CHILDREN:	*Welcome*
ANIMALS:	*Prohibited*
SMOKING:	*Prohibited*

Rhubarb Coffee Cake

Makes 8-12 servings

1/2 cup margarine, room temperature
1 1/2 cups brown sugar
1 egg
1 cup sour cream
1 teaspoon baking soda
2 cups flour
1/2 teaspoon salt
2 cups (1/2-inch cubes) rhubarb (about 3/4 pound)
1 teaspoon vanilla

Topping

1/2 cup sugar
1 teaspoon cinnamon
1 tablespoon butter
1/2 cup chopped nuts (optional)

PREHEAT OVEN TO 350°F. Grease and flour 13x9-inch glass baking dish. In a large bowl, cream together margarine and brown sugar. Add egg and blend well. Set aside. In a medium bowl, combine sour cream and baking soda. Sift flour and salt into margarine/egg mixture alternately with sour cream/baking soda mixture. Add rhubarb and vanilla. Mix well. Spoon batter into baking dish. To prepare topping, in a small bowl, combine sugar and cinnamon. Cut in butter. Add nuts, if desired. Sprinkle topping over coffee cake batter. Bake for approximately 35-40 minutes. Cool on wire rack.

> **Carol's Corner**
>
> *This yummy coffee cake also makes a great dessert. Rod loves it served warm with a big scoop of vanilla ice cream!*

B.D. Williams House

T he trademark "home away from home" breakfast at the
B. D. Williams House Bed and Breakfast delights guests' palates.
The fresh, multi-course meal features homemade muffins and breads,
cereals, juices, coffees and teas.

"Hard to be sleepless in Seattle here. It's too cozy!"

~ Guest, B.D. Williams House

INNKEEPERS:	*Susan & Doug Williams*
ADDRESS:	*1505 4th Avenue North*
	Seattle, WA 98109
TELEPHONE:	*(206) 285-0810; (800) 880-0810*
FAX:	*(206) 285-8526*
E-MAIL:	*innkeepr@wolfenet.com*
WEBSITE:	*Not Available*
ROOMS:	*5 Rooms; All with private baths*
OPEN:	*Year-round*
CHILDREN:	*Children allowed (All by prior arrangement)*
ANIMALS:	*Prohibited*
SMOKING:	*Prohibited*

Warm Prune Pecan Cake

Makes 9 servings

1 cup water
1/2 cup butter or margarine, cut into small pieces
1 cup chopped moist-pack dried prunes, pitted
1 teaspoon baking soda
1 cup sugar
1 egg
1 teaspoon vanilla
1 1/2 cups flour
1 teaspoon baking powder
3/4 cup chopped pecans

PREHEAT OVEN TO 325°F. Grease and flour a 9-inch square pan. In a medium saucepan, heat water to boiling. Remove from heat and add butter or margarine. Stir until butter is melted. Add prunes, baking soda, sugar, egg and vanilla. Beat well. Sift flour and baking powder into prune mixture. Add pecans. Blend very well. Pour batter into prepared pan. Bake for 30-35 minutes. Cut into squares and serve hot with pats of butter on each serving.

"This cake is often requested in our family for birthday breakfast."

Susan Williams - The B.D. Williams House

Camano Island Inn

Camano Island Inn

T he Camano Island Inn Bed and Breakfast boasts six deluxe waterfront guestrooms. Amenities include private baths and patios, Jacuzzi tubs and fireplaces. Each room has an unobstructed view of the boat traffic on Saratoga Passage, the Olympic Mountains and fabulous sunsets.

The apple, pear and prune orchard provides a bounty of fresh fruit used in the breakfasts.

INNKEEPERS:	*Jon & Kari Soth*
ADDRESS:	*1054 S. West Camano Drive*
	Camano Island, WA 98292
TELEPHONE:	*(360) 387-0783; (888) 718-0783*
FAX:	*(360) 387-4173*
E-MAIL:	*reservations@camanoislandinn.com*
WEBSITE:	*www.camanoislandinn.com*
ROOMS:	*6 Suites; All with private baths*
OPEN:	*Year-round*
CHILDREN:	*Well-behaved children are welcome*
ANIMALS:	*Prohibited*
SMOKING:	*Permitted outdoors only*

Cranberry-Apple Coffee Braid

Makes 8-10 servings

Dough

1 (3-ounce) package cream cheese, chilled, cut into pieces
1/4 cup (1/2 stick) butter, chilled, cut into pieces
2 cups baking mix (such as Bisquick)
1/3 cup milk

Filling

3/4 cup (8-ounces) whole berry cranberry sauce
1 large apple, peeled and chopped
1 teaspoon sugar
1/2 teaspoon cinnamon

Glaze

1 teaspoon butter, melted
1 tablespoon milk
1 tablespoon cranberry juice
1 cup powdered sugar

PREHEAT OVEN TO 425°F. Put cream cheese, butter and baking mix into a large bowl. Using a pastry blender, cut until mixture is crumbly. Blend in milk. On a floured piece of waxed paper, knead for one minute. Roll into a 14x10-inch rectangle. Remove waxed paper and place dough on a greased cookie sheet. Set aside. In a small bowl, mix together cranberry sauce, apple, sugar and cinnamon. Place cranberry mixture in a 3-inch-wide strip lengthwise down center of dough. Cut dough on both sides of filling into 1-inch-wide strips almost to filling. Alternating from side to side, fold strips over filling at an angle. End of each strip should be covered by next strip. Pinch dough at both ends to seal. Bake for 15 minutes, or until braid is golden brown. Remove to wire rack. Place a piece of waxed paper underneath rack to catch drips from the glaze.

To make glaze: In a small bowl, mix together melted butter, milk and cranberry juice. Gradually beat in powdered sugar to reach glaze consistency. Drizzle over warm braid.

Stratford Manor

S ituated on 30 acres, the Stratford Manor Bed and Breakfast is a lovely, Tudor-style country home. Guests enjoy the solarium, cozy library, enchanting gardens, elegant bath robes, fluffy towels and relaxing massages.

"A wonderful night. Far exceeded our expectations."

~ Guest, Stratford Manor

INNKEEPERS:	*Leslie & Jim Lohse*
ADDRESS:	*1416 Van Wyck Road*
	Bellingham, WA 98226
TELEPHONE:	*(360) 715-8441*
FAX:	*(360) 671-0840*
E-MAIL:	*llohse@aol.com*
WEBSITE:	*www.site-works.com/stratford*
ROOMS:	*3 Rooms; All with private baths*
OPEN:	*Year-round*
CHILDREN:	*Prohibited*
ANIMALS:	*Prohibited*
SMOKING:	*Permitted only on outside porch*

Blueberry Scones

Makes 8 scones

2 cups flour
1/4 cup sugar
1 tablespoon baking powder
1/4 teaspoon baking soda
1/4 teaspoon salt
1 tablespoon finely shredded orange peel (1-2 oranges)
1/4 cup cold, firm butter
1 cup fresh or frozen blueberries
1 egg (or 1/4 cup egg product)
1/2 cup buttermilk
1 teaspoon vanilla

PREHEAT OVEN TO 400°F. In a large bowl, sift together flour, sugar, baking powder, baking soda and salt. Add orange peel. Using a pastry blender, cut in butter until mixture resembles coarse crumbs. Add blueberries, tossing to coat. Make a well in center of ingredients; set aside. In a small bowl, stir together egg, buttermilk and vanilla. Pour wet ingredients into the well in the dry ingredients, stirring with fork until just moistened. Turn dough onto lightly floured board and knead lightly into a ball shape. Pat dough into a 7-inch circle and cut into 8 wedges. Transfer to an ungreased baking sheet, leaving 1 to 2-inches between wedges. Bake for 15-20 minutes, until lightly browned. Serve warm.

"These are also very tasty with just the orange zest or with fresh cranberries."

Leslie Lohse - Stratford Manor

Palisades at Dash Point

T he Palisades Bed and Breakfast at Dash Point offers a luxurious
European-style getaway. Guests enjoy a breathtaking view of
Puget Sound and the Olympic Mountain Range from their private,
three-room suite.

Conveniently located between Seattle and Tacoma, this secluded
hideaway pampers guests with thick terry robes, a sumptuous breakfast
and a licensed "on-call" masseuse.

INNKEEPERS:	*Dennis & Peggy LaPorte*
ADDRESS:	*5162 SW 311th Place*
	Federal Way, WA 98023
TELEPHONE:	*(253) 838-4376; (888) 838-4376*
FAX:	*(253) 838-1480*
E-MAIL:	*laporte2@ix.netcom.com*
WEBSITE:	*www.bbonline.com/wa/palisades*
ROOMS:	*1 Suite; Private bath*
OPEN:	*Year-round*
CHILDREN:	*Prohibited*
ANIMALS:	*Prohibited*
SMOKING:	*Prohibited*

Blueberry Scones with Vanilla Crème Filling

Makes 8 scones

2 1/4 cups flour
1 tablespoon baking powder
1/2 teaspoon salt
1/2 cup cold, firm butter or margarine
1/2 cup blueberries
1 egg
3/4 cup buttermilk
Sugar, to sprinkle on tops of scones
Vanilla Crème Filling (recipe to follow)

PREHEAT OVEN TO 350°F. In food processor, blend flour, baking powder and salt. Cut in butter or margarine, using on/off switch several times until mixture is crumbly. Put mixture in medium bowl and add blueberries; toss to coat. Set aside. In a small bowl, mix together egg and buttermilk. Add to flour/blueberry mixture. Stir gently, just until blended. Turn dough onto lightly floured surface and knead lightly a few times. Pat dough into a 6 to 7-inch round. Cut dough into 8 triangular pie-shaped wedges. Transfer to ungreased baking sheet and sprinkle tops of scones with sugar. Bake 20-25 minutes, or until puffed and golden. Cool on wire rack. Cut each scone in half horizontally and spread Vanilla Crème Filling between top and bottom halves.

Vanilla Crème Filling

1 1/4 cups powdered sugar
2 tablespoons butter, room temperature
1/2 teaspoon vanilla
1 tablespoon milk or half and half

In a small bowl, beat together all ingredients using electric mixer. Beat until smooth. A few more drops of milk may be added if a thinner spreading consistency is desired.

Highland Cottage

O riginally built in 1901, the refurbished Highland Cottage Bed and Breakfast was the elegant private residence of the distinguished George F. Ward family. The eclectic decor features a large and brilliantly colored stained glass window, decorative inlays and authentic antique furnishings.

This traditional Victorian has two spacious upstairs rooms and a self-contained cottage.

INNKEEPERS:	*Lon & Ellie Overson*
ADDRESS:	*622 Highland Avenue*
	Bremerton, WA 98337
TELEPHONE:	*(360) 373-2235*
FAX:	*Not Available*
E-MAIL:	*overson@hurricane.net*
WEBSITE:	*Not Available*
ROOMS:	*2 Rooms; 1 Cottage; Private and shared baths*
OPEN:	*Year-round*
CHILDREN:	*Well-behaved children are welcome*
ANIMALS:	*Prohibited*
SMOKING:	*Permitted outside only*

Country Scones with Devonshire Cream

Makes 10 scones

1 egg
Buttermilk, to make 1 cup (when combined with egg)
2 cups unbleached, all-purpose flour
1/4 cup sugar
2 1/2 teaspoons baking powder
1/2 teaspoon salt
6 tablespoons cold, firm butter
1/2 cup raisins or dried cranberries
1/2 cup white baking chips (morsels)
Devonshire Cream (recipe to follow)

PREHEAT OVEN TO 400°F. In a one-cup measure, slightly beat egg. Add buttermilk to fill. Set aside. In a large bowl, sift together flour, sugar, baking powder and salt. Using a pastry blender, cut in butter until mixture is crumbly. Toss in raisins (or cranberries) and baking chips. Add buttermilk mixture and stir just until dough clings together. Do not overmix! On ungreased baking sheet, drop dough by 1/4 cupfuls. Bake for 12-15 minutes, or until lightly browned. Serve with Devonshire Cream. Delicious!

Devonshire Cream

Makes about 1 cup

1 (3-ounce) package cream cheese, room temperature
1 tablespoon powdered sugar, sifted
1/2 teaspoon vanilla (or favorite flavoring)
1/3 cup whipping cream (may use up to 1/2 cup)

In a small bowl, beat together cream cheese, powdered sugar and vanilla until fluffy. Add whipping cream and beat just until spreading consistency. Do not overbeat.

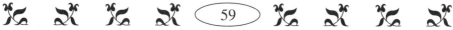

The Woodsman

Nestled on five acres amid beautiful gardens and tall trees, the Woodsman Bed and Breakfast is a peaceful getaway. The single guest room, finished entirely in cedar, offers a private bath and entrance. A delightful breakfast features freshly baked scones, breads, muffins and the day's special dish.

This welcoming retreat is a haven of privacy and tranquillity.

INNKEEPERS:	*Bill & Joyce Ostling*
ADDRESS:	*7700 Springridge Rd NE*
	Bainbridge Island, WA 98110
TELEPHONE:	*(206) 842-7386*
FAX:	*Not Available*
E-MAIL:	*Not Available*
WEBSITE:	*Not Available*
ROOMS:	*1 Room; Private bath*
OPEN:	*Year-round*
CHILDREN:	*Prohibited*
ANIMALS:	*Prohibited*
SMOKING:	*Prohibited*

Our Favorite Scones

Makes 8 scones

The "egg wash" gives these delectable scones a beautiful and shiny, browned crust.

3 cups flour
1/3 cup sugar
2 1/2 teaspoons baking powder
1/2 teaspoon baking soda
3/4 teaspoon salt
1/2 cup cold, firm butter (cut into small pieces)
1/4 cup cold, firm margarine (cut into small pieces)
1 teaspoon grated lemon peel
1 cup buttermilk
1 egg yolk
1 teaspoon water

PREHEAT OVEN TO 425°F. In a large bowl, sift together flour, sugar, baking powder, baking soda and salt. Using a pastry blender, cut in butter and margarine until mixture resembles coarse cornmeal. Stir in lemon peel and buttermilk. Turn out onto floured board and knead 12 times. Form into an 8-inch circle. Cut into 8 equal triangles (wedges) and place on ungreased baking sheet 1 1/2-inches apart. In a small bowl, beat egg yolk with water. Using a pastry brush, lightly coat the tops and sides of scones with the "egg wash". (Discard any remaining egg mixture.) Bake for 15-18 minutes, or until lightly browned. Serve warm.

Pancakes, Waffles & Blintzes

Pancakes
Waffles
&
Blintzes

Highland Guest House

O riginally built in 1902, the Highland Guest House Bed and Breakfast has been tastefully restored to capture its turn-of-the-century ambiance and is in the process of being placed on the National Register of Historic Places.

"Best B & B ever! We love it here! The owners are the greatest!"

~ Guest, Highland Guest House

INNKEEPERS: *Marilee & Brad Stolzenburg*
ADDRESS: *121 E. Highland Avenue*
Chelan, WA 98816
TELEPHONE: *(509) 682-2892; (800) 681-2892*
FAX: *Not Available*
E-MAIL: *Not Available*
WEBSITE: *www.lakechelan.com/highland.htm*
ROOMS: *2 Rooms; 1 Suite; All with private baths*
OPEN: *Year-round*
CHILDREN: *Children 10 and older are welcome*
ANIMALS: *Prohibited*
SMOKING: *Prohibited*

French Banana Pancakes

Makes 8-10 pancakes

1 cup flour
1/4 cup powdered sugar
1/4 teaspoon salt
1 cup milk
2 eggs
1/4 teaspoon vanilla
3 tablespoons butter, melted

<u>Filling</u>

1/4 cup butter, melted
1/4 cup brown sugar
1/4 teaspoon ground cinnamon
1/4 teaspoon ground nutmeg
1/4 cup light cream
5 firm bananas, halved lengthwise
Whipped cream and additional cinnamon (optional)

In a medium bowl, sift together flour, powdered sugar and salt. Add milk, eggs, vanilla and melted butter. Beat until smooth. Heat a lightly greased 6-inch skillet. Add 3 tablespoons batter to cover bottom of skillet. Cook until lightly browned; turn and brown other side. Remove to a wire rack. Repeat with remaining batter.

<u>To make filling</u>: Melt butter in large skillet. Stir in brown sugar, cinnamon and nutmeg. Add cream and cook until slightly thickened. Add bananas and heat for 2 to 3 minutes, spooning sauce over them. Remove from heat.

<u>To serve</u>: Roll a pancake around each banana half and place on serving plates. Spoon sauce over pancakes. Top with whipped cream and a dash of cinnamon.

The Victorian

L ocated in Coupeville on beautiful Whidbey Island, The Victorian Bed and Breakfast is a Registered National Historical Landmark. Guests of this Italianate Victorian home enjoy the charming upstairs bedrooms or the guest cottage.

Called the City of Sea Captains, Coupeville blends its early Indian lore with a unique maritime history and a vigorous pioneer spirit.

INNKEEPERS:	*Al & Marion Sasso*
ADDRESS:	*602 North Main Street*
	Coupeville, WA 98239
TELEPHONE:	*(360) 678-5305*
FAX:	*Not Available*
E-MAIL:	*Not Available*
WEBSITE:	*www.whidbey.net/~asasso/*
ROOMS:	*2 Rooms; 1 Cottage; All with private baths*
OPEN:	*February through December*
CHILDREN:	*Children are welcome in the cottage*
ANIMALS:	*Animals are allowed in the cottage*
SMOKING:	*Prohibited*

Apple Pancake

Makes 6-8 servings

8 eggs
1 1/2 cups milk
3 tablespoons sugar
1 teaspoon vanilla
1/2 teaspoon salt
1/2 teaspoon cinnamon
1/2 cup (1 stick) margarine, cut into pieces
2 large Granny Smith apples
1 cup flour
4 tablespoons brown sugar

PREHEAT OVEN TO 425°F. In a large bowl, mix together eggs, milk, sugar, vanilla, salt and cinnamon. Set aside. In the oven, melt margarine in a 13x9-inch baking dish. (Watch carefully so it doesn't burn.) Peel apples and cut into 1/4-inch slices and arrange in dish. Stir flour into egg/milk mixture; it will be lumpy. Return dish with margarine and apples to oven until margarine sizzles. Remove dish from oven and pour batter over apples. Sprinkle with brown sugar and return to oven. (Use potholders, as dish will still be hot!) Bake for 25 minutes. Serve immediately.

Otters Pond

S ituated on six and one-half acres on breathtaking Orcas Island, the Otters Pond Bed and Breakfast overlooks a 20-acre pond. The pond attracts a multitude of wildlife that includes otters, ducks, geese, blue heron, kingfishers, bald eagles and trumpeter swans. Sports enthusiasts enjoy biking, hiking, kayaking, fishing or searching for Orcas whales.

Each guest room highlights original artwork from local artists.

INNKEEPERS:	*Carl & Susan Silvernail*
ADDRESS:	*6 Pond Road; PO Box 1540*
	Eastsound, WA 98245
TELEPHONE:	*(360) 376-8844; (888) 893-9680*
FAX:	*(360) 376-8847*
E-MAIL:	*otterbehere@otterspond.com*
WEBSITE:	*www.otterspond.com*
ROOMS:	*4 Rooms; Private and shared baths*
OPEN:	*Year-round*
CHILDREN:	*Prohibited*
ANIMALS:	*Prohibited*
SMOKING:	*Prohibited*

Yummy Apple Pancakes from the Great Northwest

Makes 10 pancakes

5 tablespoons butter, melted
1 cup milk
2 eggs
1 apple, peeled and cored, diced or sliced thinly
1 1/4 cups flour
1/2 teaspoon salt
4 teaspoons baking powder
2 tablespoons sugar
1 teaspoon cinnamon
Apple-Raisin Topping (recipe to follow)
1 cup coarsely chopped toasted walnuts (directions below)
Maple syrup

In a medium bowl, beat together melted butter, milk and eggs. Stir in apples. Set aside. In a large bowl, sift together flour, salt, baking powder, sugar and cinnamon. Gently add milk/egg mixture to flour mixture, and stir only until dry ingredients are moistened. Cook on an oiled, hot griddle or skillet, using 1/4 cup batter for each pancake. Serve with Apple-Raisin Topping, toasted walnuts and maple syrup.

Apple-Raisin Topping

Makes about 2 1/2 cups topping

1 (21-ounce) can apple pie filling/topping
1/4 cup brown sugar
1/4 cup dried cranberries
1/4 cup raisins
1/4 cup golden raisins

In a medium saucepan, mix together all ingredients. Cook on medium heat until warm and bubbly. Thin with a little water if mixture seems too thick. Serve on pancakes, or put topping in a bowl for guests to serve themselves.

To toast walnuts: Bake nuts on an ungreased cookie sheet at 350°F., checking every few minutes until they turn a light brown. Serve on pancakes, or put nuts in a bowl for guests to serve themselves.

Chestnut Hill Inn

T he Chestnut Hill Inn Bed and Breakfast is nestled in a picturesque valley on Orcas Island in spectacular Puget Sound. Guests awaken to the aroma of home-baked breads, fresh ground coffee and views of rustic stables and an evergreen forest.

For an extended summer adventure or a romantic winter retreat, this grand estate provides the perfect setting.

INNKEEPERS:	*Daniel & Marilyn Loewke*
ADDRESS:	*PO Box 213*
	Orcas, WA 98280
TELEPHONE:	*(360) 376-5157*
FAX:	*(360) 376-5283*
E-MAIL:	*chestnut@pacificrim.net*
WEBSITE:	*www.chestnuthillinn.com*
ROOMS:	*4 Rooms; 1 Suite; 1 Cottage; All with private baths*
OPEN:	*Year-round*
CHILDREN:	*Children 13 and older are welcome (Call ahead)*
ANIMALS:	*Prohibited; Resident cats and dogs*
SMOKING:	*Prohibited*

Polish Apple Pancakes with Marionberry Butter

Makes 4 servings (about 10 pancakes)

1 cup flour
1 tablespoon sugar
1/2 teaspoon salt
1 egg
1 cup milk
1 tablespoon oil
3 tablespoons butter
5 medium apples, cored, peeled and thinly sliced
1/4 cup brown sugar
Marionberry butter (recipe to follow)
Powdered sugar
Maple syrup

Using a food processor, combine flour, sugar, salt, egg, milk and oil. Blend until smooth, about 1 minute. Pour batter into large bowl and set aside. In heavy skillet, melt butter and add apples. Sprinkle with brown sugar and sauté for about 2 minutes or until slightly cooked. Strain off excess liquid. Add apples to batter; blend until apples are completely coated. (If not going to make pancakes right away, cover with plastic wrap so air does not affect color of apples.) On a lightly greased hot griddle or skillet, pour batter by 1/4-cupfuls and spread to form a 5-inch circle. When surface is no longer shiny, turn and cook the other side until apples are semi-soft and pancakes are golden brown. Serve with marionberry butter and a dusting of powdered sugar, and offer maple syrup on the side.

Marionberry Butter

Butter, room temperature
Marionberry jam (use your favorite "no seed" jam or preserves if marionberry is not available)

In food processor, whip butter until smooth. Add jam to taste and whip some more.

Blue Heron Inn

L ocated opposite the Mount St. Helens National Monument, the Blue Heron Inn features six beautiful rooms with private bathrooms and balconies. Guests relax in the spacious parlor with its breathtaking views of Silver Lake and Mount St. Helens or browse through the library with its fine selection of books and other reading material.

A savory country breakfast and full-course dinner is provided for all guests.

INNKEEPERS:	*John & Jeanne Robards*
ADDRESS:	*2846 Spirit Lake Hwy*
	Castle Rock, WA 98611
TELEPHONE:	*(360) 274-9595; (800) 959-4049*
FAX:	*Not Available*
E-MAIL:	*jeanne@blueheroninn.com*
WEBSITE:	*www.blueheroninn.com*
ROOMS:	*6 Rooms; All with private baths*
OPEN:	*Year-round*
CHILDREN:	*Children over the age of 6 are welcome*
ANIMALS:	*Prohibited*
SMOKING:	*Permitted outside on decks and patios*

Sourdough Pancakes

Makes 20 (5-inch) pancakes

No mess and no fuss in the morning! Make this pancake batter ahead of time. Batter keeps for days!

1 package active dry yeast
1/4 cup warm water
4 cups (1 quart) buttermilk
1/2 cup vegetable oil
1 teaspoon salt
4 tablespoons sugar
1 tablespoon baking soda
4 cups flour
2 tablespoons baking powder
4 eggs, well beaten

In a very large bowl, dissolve yeast in warm water. Stir in buttermilk, oil, salt, sugar and baking soda. Add flour and baking powder; mix well. Fold in eggs. Store in refrigerator overnight in container at least 2 times bigger than amount of mixture. (Don't worry about a dark film that will grow on top of batter; be sure to stir it in before using.) Batter will keep in refrigerator for up to 2 weeks.

To make pancakes: Drop batter by 1/3-cupfuls onto a hot, oiled griddle or skillet. Cook until golden brown on each side.

Salisbury House

S alisbury House Bed and Breakfast Inn offers gracious accommodations for the discerning traveler. Situated on a tree-lined residential
street, this urban bed and breakfast is only minutes from downtown
Seattle, the University of Washington and Seattle University.

The public rooms are large and bright. A well-stocked library has a
game table for an evening of chess or a morning of writing postcards by
the fire.

INNKEEPERS:	*Cathryn & Mary Wiese*
ADDRESS:	*750 16th Avenue East*
	Seattle, WA 98112
TELEPHONE:	*(206) 328-8682*
FAX:	*(206) 720-1019*
E-MAIL:	*cathy@salisburyhouse.com*
WEBSITE:	*www.salisburyhouse.com*
ROOMS:	*4 Rooms; All with private baths*
OPEN:	*Year-round*
CHILDREN:	*Children over the age of 12 are welcome*
ANIMALS:	*Prohibited*
SMOKING:	*Prohibited*

Mary's Oatmeal Pancakes

Makes 4-6 servings, about 20 (4-inch) pancakes

For these surprisingly light and fluffy pancakes, the oats soak in buttermilk overnight so they offer body, texture, and richness to the batter, without weighing it down. They are delicious served with a side of chunky applesauce; see Mary's recipe on page 163.

2 cups rolled oats
3 cups buttermilk
1/2 cup flour
1 teaspoon baking soda
1 teaspoon baking powder
1/4 teaspoon salt
2 eggs, lightly beaten
1/4 cup vegetable oil
Maple syrup (topping)
Low-fat sour cream (topping)
Yogurt (topping)

The night before making pancakes, in a large bowl, stir together oats and buttermilk. Cover and refrigerate overnight. When ready to make pancakes, in a large bowl, combine flour, baking soda, baking powder and salt. Set aside. In a small bowl, stir together eggs and oil. Add egg mixture to flour mixture, followed by the oatmeal mixture. Stir gently until thoroughly combined. Cook the pancakes on lightly oiled, hot griddle or skillet until golden brown, about 2 minutes per side. Serve hot, topped with real maple syrup and a combination of low-fat sour cream and yogurt, and chunky applesauce on the side.

Carol's Corner

To save time in the morning, all three mixtures can be prepared the night before and set aside. (Refrigerate the egg and oil mixture.)

Granny Sandy's Orchard

L ocated near the Olympic National Park, Granny Sandy's Orchard Bed and Breakfast is a bird watcher's haven. Among the usual robins, chickadees, house finches and starlings, a piebald robin and hairy woodpecker have been spotted under the trees.

Many of the exceptionally luscious meals feature fruit from Granny's orchard. Recent additions to the orchard include plum, peach and apricot trees.

INNKEEPERS: *Sandy & Paul Moore*
ADDRESS: *405 West Spruce*
Sequim, WA 98382
TELEPHONE: *(360) 683-5748*
FAX: *(360) 683-4365*
E-MAIL: *moorross@olypen.com*
WEBSITE: *www.olypen.com/moorross/*
ROOMS: *2 Rooms; Both with private baths*
OPEN: *Year-round*
CHILDREN: *Welcome (Call ahead for guidelines)*
ANIMALS: *Prohibited*
SMOKING: *Prohibited*

Potato Pancakes

Makes 1 serving, about 4 (4-inch) thin pancakes

Ingredients can be easily doubled or tripled.

1 medium potato, grated
1 tablespoon onion, finely chopped
1 teaspoon flour
1/4 teaspoon baking powder
1 egg, lightly beaten
1 teaspoon sour cream
1 tablespoon chopped pecans
1 tablespoon vegetable oil

In a medium bowl, combine potato and onion. Mix in flour and baking powder. Add egg, sour cream and pecans. Mix thoroughly. Heat oil in skillet over medium to medium-high heat. Spread batter thinly and cook until bottom of pancake is very crisp, about 5-6 minutes. Loosen edges, turn and cook other side until crisp.

Serving suggestion: Potato Pancakes are great with butter, maple syrup, applesauce, sausage or bacon.

Inn at Penn Cove

T he Inn at Penn Cove Bed and Breakfast consists of two of Coupeville's finest historic homes: the 1887 Kineth House and the 1891 Coupe-Gillespie House. The Italianate Kineth House, listed on the National Registry, has an air of quiet luxury. The Coupe-Gillespie combines a fresh country feel with touches of Oriental beauty.

The inn is located on Whidbey Island, the longest island on the US Pacific Coast.

INNKEEPERS:	*Mitchell & Gladys Howard*
ADDRESS:	*702 North Main Street*
	Coupeville, WA 98239
TELEPHONE:	*(360) 678-8000; (800) 688-2683*
FAX:	*Not Available*
E-MAIL:	*penncove@whidbey.net*
WEBSITE:	*www.whidbey.net/~penncove/pencv.htm*
ROOMS:	*6 Rooms; Private and shared baths*
OPEN:	*Year-round*
CHILDREN:	*Welcome (Call ahead for guidelines)*
ANIMALS:	*Prohibited*
SMOKING:	*Prohibited*

Rice Pancakes

Makes 8 pancakes

This recipe is simple and can also be modified to meet several unusual diets. It is low in fat and sodium, and the flour can be replaced by rice flour or any gluten-free flour for those who are gluten intolerant.

2 tablespoons flour
1 teaspoon baking powder
2 eggs (if egg-replacers are used, pancakes may not hold together very well)
2 tablespoons skim milk
2 tablespoons canola oil
1 1/2 cups cooked brown rice

In a medium bowl, mix together flour and baking powder. Set aside. In another medium bowl, beat together eggs, milk and oil. Stir in rice. Add wet ingredients to dry ingredients. Mix until combined. Drop batter by scant 1/4-cupfuls and cook on a hot griddle or a nonstick frying pan.

> **Carol's Corner**
>
> *I tested this recipe using a nonstick frying pan. The pancakes browned nicely using no additional oil.*

MacKaye Harbor Inn

The MacKaye Harbor Inn was originally built in 1904 by the Tralness family. In 1927, while Mr. and Mrs. Tralness visited family in Norway, their teenage children rebuilt the old farmhouse. It became the first home on Lopez Island to have electricity.

Hospitality has pervaded this island getaway. Mrs. Tralness kept Norwegian cookies in the entry for passersby, and its sandy beach was the site of many island picnics.

INNKEEPERS:	*Robin & Mike Bergstrom*
ADDRESS:	*Route 1, PO Box 1940*
	Lopez Island, WA 98261
TELEPHONE:	*(360) 468-2253*
FAX:	*(360) 468-2393*
E-MAIL:	*mckay@pacificrim.net*
WEBSITE:	*www.pacificrim.net/~mckay*
ROOMS:	*4 Rooms; 1 Suite; 2 Cottages; Private and shared baths*
OPEN:	*Year-round*
CHILDREN:	*Children nine and older are welcome*
ANIMALS:	*Prohibited*
SMOKING:	*Prohibited*

Finnish Pancake

Makes 6-8 servings

8 eggs
1/2 teaspoon salt
1/4 cup honey
2/3 cup flour
2 1/2 cups milk
4 tablespoons butter
Suggested toppings: jam, powdered sugar or nutmeg

PREHEAT OVEN TO 425°F. In a blender, combine eggs, salt and honey. Alternately, add flour and milk, blending after each addition. In the oven, melt the butter in a 13x9-inch baking dish. Check butter <u>frequently</u> so it doesn't burn. Pour batter over melted butter in preheated baking dish. Return to oven (use potholders!) and bake for 20-25 minutes, or until puffed and golden. Drizzle with hot, melted jam or sprinkle with powdered sugar or nutmeg.

"This is the recipe that gets the best reviews and, therefore, has become our benchmark or tradition at the inn. It's almost like having custard for breakfast, something gentle for the awakening tummy and tongue."

Robin Bergstrom - MacKaye Harbor Inn

Kangaroo House

S ince 1953, when Captain Ferris returned from Australia with a young kangaroo, this lovely home has been known as the Kangaroo House. Guests find a restful haven of lovely gardens, delicious breakfasts and delightfully decorated and comfortable rooms.

Breakfast ingredients include the freshest of seasonal fruits, vegetables, garden herbs and local specialties. All breads, pastries and muffins are baked in the kitchen.

INNKEEPERS:	*Peter & Helen Allen*
ADDRESS:	*5 North Beach Road, Orcas Island*
	Eastsound, WA 98245
TELEPHONE:	*(360) 376-2175; (888) 371-2175*
FAX:	*(360) 376-3604*
E-MAIL:	*kangaroo@thesanjuans.com*
WEBSITE:	*www.pacificws.com/kangaroo*
ROOMS:	*4 Rooms; 1 Suite; Private and shared baths*
OPEN:	*Year-round*
CHILDREN:	*Children of all ages are welcome*
ANIMALS:	*Prohibited*
SMOKING:	*Prohibited*

Cornmeal Yeast Waffles

Makes 6-10 waffles (depends on size/shape of waffle iron)

Plan ahead! For a special waffle treat in the morning, you must start making the batter the night before.

2 cups milk
1 package (2 1/4 teaspoons) active dry yeast
1/2 cup warm water (105–115°F.)
1/3 cup butter or margarine, melted
1 teaspoon salt
1 tablespoon sugar
2 cups flour
1 cup yellow corn meal
2 large eggs, slightly beaten
1/2 teaspoon baking soda

In a medium saucepan, scald milk and set aside. Cool to lukewarm (105-115°F.) In a very large bowl, sprinkle yeast into warm water. Stir until yeast is dissolved. (Note: Depending on overnight kitchen temperature, the yeast mixture may double in size. Be sure to use a bowl large enough to allow for this growth. Nobody wants to find a mess in the kitchen first thing in the morning!) Add lukewarm milk, butter, salt, sugar, flour and corn meal. Mix until batter is smooth. Cover and let stand at room temperature overnight. In the morning, add eggs and baking soda. Beat well. Bake waffles in a preheated, lightly greased waffle iron.

> **⅞ Carol's Corner**
>
> *Baked waffles may be transferred to a 200°F. oven, placing them directly on the oven rack. This will keep them crisp and hot while the rest of the waffles are baked. Everyone can eat at once, including the cook!*

Bellingham's DeCann House

Built at the turn-of-the-century, Bellingham's DeCann House Bed and Breakfast overlooks Bellingham Bay and the San Juan Islands. Located approximately one hour from both Seattle, Washington and Vancouver, British Columbia, this restored grand old home is decorated with family heirlooms.

Guests enjoy a savory breakfast that features Aunt Van's special egg dishes or fruit specialties.

INNKEEPERS:	*Barbara and Van Hudson*
ADDRESS:	*2610 Eldridge Avenue*
	Bellingham, WA 98225
TELEPHONE:	*(360) 734-9172*
FAX:	*Not Available*
E-MAIL:	*hudson@pacificrim.net*
WEBSITE:	*www.pacificrim.net/~hudson*
ROOMS:	*2 Rooms; Both with private baths*
OPEN:	*Open Thanksgiving through December*
CHILDREN:	*Children over the age of 12 are welcome*
ANIMALS:	*Prohibited*
SMOKING:	*Permitted outside on covered porches*

Oatmeal Waffles

Makes about 8 waffles (depends on size/shape of waffle iron)

1 1/2 cups flour
1 cup quick-cooking oats
1 tablespoon baking powder
1/2 teaspoon cinnamon
1/4 teaspoon salt (optional)
2 eggs, slightly beaten
1 1/2 cups milk
6 tablespoons butter, melted
2 tablespoons brown sugar
Peaches and vanilla yogurt (optional)

In a large bowl, stir together flour, oats, baking powder, cinnamon and salt; set aside. In a small bowl, stir together eggs, milk, butter and brown sugar. Add wet ingredients to flour mixture and stir until well blended. Pour batter onto preheated, lightly greased waffle iron. Close lid and do not open until waffles are finished.

<u>Serving suggestion</u>: Oatmeal Waffles are wonderful topped with home canned peaches and vanilla yogurt.

"This is one of several recipes passed on by friends. Our neighbor gave us this one not only because it is delicious, but because it is from a cookbook of food for diabetics which means it's also good for you."

Barb and Van Hudson - Bellingham's DeCann House

Salisbury House

B uilt in 1904, the Salisbury House has been an urban bed and breakfast inn since 1985. The public rooms are large and bright. A full breakfast that features luscious seasonal fruits and delectable breads and muffins is served in the sunny dining room.

The four guest rooms are each individually decorated and have private baths. Certain rooms have cushioned window seats and walk-in closets.

INNKEEPERS:	*Cathryn & Mary Wiese*
ADDRESS:	*750 16th Avenue East*
	Seattle, WA 98112
TELEPHONE:	*(206) 328-8682*
FAX:	*(206) 720-1019*
E-MAIL:	*cathy@salisburyhouse.com*
WEBSITE:	*www.salisburyhouse.com*
ROOMS:	*4 Rooms; All with private baths*
OPEN:	*Year-round*
CHILDREN:	*Children over the age of 12 are welcome*
ANIMALS:	*Prohibited*
SMOKING:	*Prohibited*

Baked Blintz

Makes 8 servings

This is much easier than filling individual crépes. A great recipe to use when entertaining a group!

Filling

1 (8-ounce) package cream cheese, room temperature
1 cup low-fat, small curd cottage cheese
1 egg, beaten
1 tablespoon sugar
1 teaspoon vanilla

Batter

1/2 cup (1 stick) butter or margarine, room temperature
1/3 cup sugar
4 eggs
1 cup flour
2 teaspoons baking powder
1 cup plain yogurt
1/2 cup low-fat sour cream
1/2 cup orange juice
Suggested toppings: Sour cream, yogurt, fresh berry preserves, fresh
    raspberries or cherry pie filling

PREHEAT OVEN TO 375°F. Butter and flour a 13x9-inch baking dish. To make filling: In a small bowl, combine cream cheese, cottage cheese, egg, sugar and vanilla. Beat well and set aside. To make batter: In a large bowl, cream together butter and sugar. Add eggs, one at a time, beating well after each addition. Stir in flour and baking powder. Mix in yogurt, sour cream and orange juice. To make blintz: Pour 1/2 of batter into prepared baking dish. Spoon the filling mixture on top of the batter, then pour remaining batter over all. Bake for 45-50 minutes, or until lightly browned. Cut into squares and serve with a dollop of sour cream, yogurt, fresh berry preserves, fresh raspberries or cherry pie filling.

"Over the years this has been one of our most requested recipes. It makes a great brunch dish and it can be assembled the night before, refrigerated and baked in the morning."

Cathryn and Mary Wiese - Salisbury House

Chinaberry Hill

P erched on a hill overlooking Puget Sound, Chinaberry Hill is a remarkable garden retreat that works its magic on anyone who enters. Examples of unexpected whimsical combinations found throughout the house include a primitive chest surrounded with fiberglass chicken weather vanes, art deco theater curtains and a buzz-saw fishing bear.

This 1889 Victorian is on the National Register of Historic Places.

INNKEEPERS:	*Cecil & Yarrow Wayman*
ADDRESS:	*302 Tacoma Avenue North*
	North Tacoma, WA 98403
TELEPHONE:	*(253) 272-1282*
FAX:	*(253) 272-1335*
E-MAIL:	*chinaberry@wa.net*
WEBSITE:	*www.wa.net/chinaberry*
ROOMS:	*1 Room; 4 Suites; All with private baths*
OPEN:	*Year-round*
CHILDREN:	*Children are welcome in the guest cottage*
ANIMALS:	*Prohibited; Resident cats*
SMOKING:	*Permitted on outside verandah*

Bernie's Zucchini-Cheddar Blintzes

Makes 10 blintzes

1 cup baking mix (Cecil uses Krusteaz pancake mix)
1 cup milk
1 egg
1 cup grated zucchini
1 cup extra sharp cheddar cheese
1 teaspoon vanilla
Whipped cream cheese or vanilla yogurt
Cherry preserves or your favorite fruit preserve

Preheat lightly oiled griddle to 350°F., or heat a lightly oiled skillet over medium-high heat. In a large bowl, using a wire whisk, combine baking mix, milk, egg, zucchini, cheddar cheese and vanilla. Mix thoroughly. Drop batter by 1/4-cupfuls (blintzes will be about 4-inches in diameter) onto griddle. Turn blintzes over when edges begin to dry. After cooking about two minutes longer, transfer blintzes to serving plates. Spread 1 to 2 tablespoons of cream cheese or yogurt on each blintz, roll up and top with preserves.

<u>Serving suggestion</u>: These are incredible with heated, thinly sliced ham. For a completely different experience, try using even more of the shredded cheese as a filling and serve with spicy, hot applesauce.

"The guest who gave us this recipe is credited in the name. Thicker than a normal blintz, they are also highly aromatic, turn a golden brown, and draw rave reviews whenever they are served. Best of all, they are quick, simple and extremely filling."

Cecil Wayman - Chinaberry Hill

French Toast, Granola & Oatmeal

French Toast

Granola

&

Oatmeal

Highland Guest House

S ituated on the north shore of Lake Chelan, the Highland Guest House
Bed and Breakfast was originally built in 1902 and has been
tastefully restored to capture its original charm. Many of the country
and Victorian collectibles featured throughout this enchanting home can
be purchased.

The Rose and Wicker Room features white wicker beds and hand-
stenciled walls. Decorated in a French country theme, this cozy room
offers a private porch and a Victorian-style bathroom.

INNKEEPERS:	*Marilee & Brad Stolzenburg*
ADDRESS:	*121 East Highland Avenue*
	Chelan, WA 98816
TELEPHONE:	*(509) 682-2892; (800) 681-2892*
FAX:	*Not Available*
E-MAIL:	*Not Available*
WEBSITE:	*www.lakechelan.com/highland.htm*
ROOMS:	*2 Rooms; 1 Suite; All with private baths*
OPEN:	*Year-round*
CHILDREN:	*Children 10 and older are welcome*
ANIMALS:	*Prohibited*
SMOKING:	*Prohibited*

Highland Raspberry and Cream French Toast

Makes 2 servings

Plan ahead for this one! Soak the bread overnight or at least several hours before cooking.

3 large eggs
3/4 cup half-and-half
6 slices French bread, sliced 1/2-inch thick
1/2 cup (1 stick) butter, melted
1/2 cup frozen freezer raspberry jam, or any other favorite flavor
   (recipe for freezer jam can be found inside box of liquid
   fruit pectin)
2 tablespoons butter, for griddle
Powdered sugar, for garnish
Fresh fruit, for garnish

In small bowl, mix together eggs and half-and-half. Blend well. Place bread slices in an ungreased 11x7-inch baking dish. Pour egg mixture evenly over bread. Cover and refrigerate for several hours or overnight until liquid is absorbed.

To make sauce: In a small bowl, mix together melted butter and jam until well combined. Set aside until ready to serve. (The sauce can be prepared in advance and refrigerated.)

To prepare French toast: PREHEAT GRIDDLE TO 350°F. Melt 2 table-spoons butter on griddle and cook bread slices for approximately 8 minutes each side. Warm sauce, stirring well, and drizzle over French toast. Sprinkle with powdered sugar. Garnish with fresh fruit on top.

"We have been serving this French toast for eight years, and people return and ask for their favorite fruit flavor."

Marilee Stolzenburg - Highland Guest House

Caswell's on the Bay

P rivacy is a main feature of Caswell's on the Bay Bed and Breakfast Inn. The guest rooms are decorated with antiques and have either a water or garden view. The finest Caswell-Massey bath amenities are provided.

"Good birding! Good relaxing! Great weekend!"

~ Guest, Caswell's on the Bay

INNKEEPERS:	*Bob & Marilyn Caswell*
ADDRESS:	*25204 Sandridge Road*
	Ocean Park, WA 98640
TELEPHONE:	*(360) 665-6535*
FAX:	*(360) 665-6500*
E-MAIL:	*Not Available*
WEBSITE:	*www.site-works.com/caswells*
ROOMS:	*5 Rooms; All with private baths*
OPEN:	*Year-round*
CHILDREN:	*Children over the age of 12 are welcome*
ANIMALS:	*Prohibited*
SMOKING:	*Permitted outside only*

Baked Orange Pecan French Toast

Makes 4-6 servings

A great make-ahead recipe! Soak the French bread in an orange flavored mixture the night before, and pop it in the oven in the morning. Easy, yet elegant!

6 eggs
2/3 cup orange juice
1/3 cup milk
3 tablespoons orange liqueur
1/4 cup sugar
1 tablespoon grated orange peel (zest)
1/2 teaspoon vanilla
1/4 teaspoon ground nutmeg
12 slices French bread, thick sliced
1/3 cup butter, melted
1/2 cup chopped pecans
Powdered sugar, for garnish
Fresh fruit, for garnish
Syrup

In a large bowl, whisk or beat together eggs, orange juice, milk, orange liqueur, sugar, orange peel, vanilla and nutmeg. Dip each slice of French bread in mixture to coat both sides. Place soaked bread slices in a single layer on an ungreased 10x15-inch jelly-roll pan. Pour any remaining mixture over bread. Cover with plastic wrap and refrigerate overnight.

Next morning: PREHEAT OVEN TO 375°F. Divide melted butter evenly between two 13x9-inch glass baking dishes and spread to completely cover bottom of dishes. Place soaked bread slices in a single layer in the two dishes and sprinkle with pecans. Bake on middle rack in oven for 20 minutes. Do not turn slices over. If crisper French toast is desired, turn oven up to 400°F. and bake for 10 minutes longer, or until crisp and golden brown. Remove from baking dishes to warm plates. Sprinkle with powdered sugar and garnish with fresh fruit. Offer variety of syrups.

> ### Carol's Corner
> *Our friends, Denny, Sue, Steve and Debbie, gave this flavorful French toast a "10" at a recipe-testing brunch. I think you will, too!*

Harbor Hill

C harm and comfort await guests of the Harbor Hill Inn Bed and Breakfast. This 1908 manor house was built by one of Everett's pioneer lumber mill owners. The Captain's Room has a queen-sized bed surrounded by ship paintings, fishing items, collectibles and oriental rugs. The Sewing Room features old sewing machines, patchwork quilts and handmade crafts.

The nearby Everett marina offers charter salmon fishing, harbor and San Juan Island tours.

INNKEEPERS:	*Larry & Sue Deisher*
ADDRESS:	*2208 Rucker Avenue*
	Everett, WA 98201
TELEPHONE:	*(425) 259-3925; (888) 572-3925*
FAX:	*(425) 258-5096*
E-MAIL:	*Not Available*
WEBSITE:	*Not Available*
ROOMS:	*5 Rooms; All with private baths*
OPEN:	*Year-round*
CHILDREN:	*Children are allowed with prior arrangement*
ANIMALS:	*Prohibited*
SMOKING:	*Permitted on outside decks only*

Creamy Sunshine French Toast

Makes 8 servings

Filling

1 (8-ounce) tub of regular cream cheese
3/4 cup orange marmalade

Batter

4 eggs
3/4 cup milk
1/4 cup half-and-half
1 tablespoon orange liqueur (or orange extract)
1 tablespoon sugar
1/4 teaspoon ground nutmeg
16 slices cinnamon raisin bread
Butter or oil (to grease pan)
Powdered sugar, orange slices and mint, for garnish

To prepare filling: In a small bowl, gently mix together cream cheese and marmalade. Set aside. To make batter: In a medium bowl, beat together eggs, milk, half-and-half, orange liqueur or extract, sugar and nutmeg. Set aside. To make French toast "sandwiches": Spread small amount of filling on 8 slices of raisin bread. Top with remaining slices of bread. Heat greased skillet over medium heat. Dip each sandwich lightly in batter one or two times coating each side. Fry sandwiches, turning 3 or 4 times to brown sides, but keeping filling from melting. To serve: Slice French toast in halves or quarters, sprinkle with powdered sugar and garnish with orange slices and fresh mint.

"Our guests enjoy the creamy citrus flavor and the different bread choice of this French toast. This is an excellent recipe for those mornings when guests have different time schedules. It can be prepared quickly and served fresh each time. The ingredients can be kept on-hand for drop-in guests and makes a wonderful presentation."

Sue Deisher - Harbor Hill Inn

> ### Carol's Corner
>
> *This is a perfect recipe! It's easy, flavorful and beautiful to serve! If you wish, make the filling mixture and batter mixture the night before and refrigerate. In the morning, all you have to do is spread the filling, fry the French toast...and you're done!*

Chambered Nautilus

Breakfast at the Chambered Nautilus Bed and Breakfast Inn is an elegant event in the antique-furnished dining room, complete with its own fireplace. Guests are treated to fresh fruit, juice, granola, baked goods and mouth-watering entrées such as Northwest Salmon Breakfast Pie or Stuffed French Toast with Homemade Orange Syrup.

Well-maintained trails and parks are nearby for walkers, joggers and bicyclists.

INNKEEPERS:	*Joyce Schulte & Steven Poole*
ADDRESS:	*5005 22nd Avenue NE*
	Seattle, WA 98105
TELEPHONE:	*(206) 522-2536; (800) 545-8459*
FAX:	*(206) 528-0898*
E-MAIL:	*chamberednautilus@msn.com*
WEBSITE:	*www.virtualcities.com*
ROOMS:	*6 Rooms; All with private baths*
OPEN:	*Year-round*
CHILDREN:	*Children 8 and older are welcome with prior arrangement*
ANIMALS:	*Prohibited*
SMOKING:	*Prohibited*

Stuffed French Toast with Orange Syrup

Makes 4 servings (2 slices each)

8 slices French bread, sliced 1-inch thick
4 ounces cream cheese, room temperature
1/4 cup orange marmalade
3 eggs
3/4 cup milk
1/4 teaspoon vanilla
1/8 teaspoon cinnamon
Dash ground nutmeg
2 tablespoons butter or margarine
Powdered sugar, for garnish
Orange slices, for garnish
Orange syrup (recipe to follow)

With the point of a sharp knife, in each slice of bread, make a slit in the center of the top crust cutting down a couple inches to make a "pocket". In a small bowl, stir together cream cheese and marmalade just until combined (overstirring causes mixture to become too soupy). Spoon about 1 tablespoon cream cheese mixture into each pocket. In a medium bowl, beat together eggs, milk, vanilla, cinnamon and nutmeg. Dip stuffed bread slices into egg mixture. Melt butter on griddle or in a skillet over medium heat. Cook stuffed bread slices until golden brown on each side, turning once. Sprinkle with powdered sugar, garnish with an orange slice and serve with orange syrup.

Orange Syrup

Makes about 2 cups

1 cup sugar
1 cup (2 sticks) butter
1 (6-ounce) can frozen orange juice concentrate

In small saucepan, combine sugar, butter and orange juice concentrate. Place over low heat until butter and frozen orange juice are melted. Do not boil. Remove from heat and cool for 5-10 minutes. Beat until slightly thickened and serve warm. Make-ahead tip: Orange syrup will keep in refrigerator for several weeks. When ready to serve, just reheat in microwave until melted and warm. Do not overheat.

Carol's Corner

A double dose of orange flavor! A delicious orange syrup complements the orange marmalade and cream cheese filling in this delectable French toast.

Inn at Swifts Bay

S ince 1988, the Inn at Swifts Bay has been recognized as one of the finest bed and breakfasts in the San Juan Islands. Nestled between Swifts Bay and the Shoal Bay, this private getaway boasts a "weekend in the country" ambiance.

Guests rave about the unique, gourmet breakfasts that excite their palates with the delectable flavors of the Pacific Northwest.

INNKEEPERS:	*Rob Aney, Carol & Tim Ortner, Margie Zener*
	Owners: Rob Aney & Mark Adcock
ADDRESS:	*Route 2, PO Box 3402*
	Lopez Island, WA 98261
TELEPHONE:	*(360) 468-3636*
FAX:	*(360) 468-3637*
E-MAIL:	*inn@swiftsbay.com*
WEBSITE:	*www.swiftsbay.com*
ROOMS:	*5 Rooms; 3 Suites; Private and shared baths*
OPEN:	*Year-round*
CHILDREN:	*Prohibited*
ANIMALS:	*Prohibited*
SMOKING:	*Prohibited*

Orange Bread Pudding French Toast

Makes 2 loaves, each loaf serves 6 (2 slices per person)

Make-ahead tip: The bread pudding is best if made a day or two before making the French toast. The orange custard sauce may also be made in advance.

Bread Pudding

1 loaf (1 3/4 to 2 lbs.) orange bread (or French bread), cut into 1-inch cubes
1 cup chopped walnuts
1 tablespoon grated orange peel (zest)
1 teaspoon ground cinnamon
1/4 teaspoon ground cloves
2 cups whole milk
2 cups half-and-half
5 large eggs
1/2 cup sugar
1 teaspoon vanilla
Sugar/cinnamon mixture (2 t. sugar and 1/2 t. cinnamon)

Orange Custard Sauce

Makes 3 cups

1 cup heavy cream
1 cup whole milk
5 egg yolks
1/2 cup sugar
1/4 cup orange syrup (the kind used to flavor coffee and Italian sodas)

French Toast Mixture

4 eggs
1/2 cup half-and-half

PREHEAT OVEN TO 350°F. Grease two 9x5-inch loaf pans. In a large bowl, combine bread cubes, nuts, orange zest, cinnamon and cloves. In a medium saucepan, combine milk and half-and-half; heat until just ready to boil. Remove from heat. In a medium bowl, whisk together eggs and sugar until light colored. Gradually add hot milk mixture to eggs. Add vanilla. Arrange bread cube mixture in loaf pans, gently pressing cubes to fit. Pour milk mixture slowly over bread, allowing time for bread to absorb liquid. Sprinkle sugar/cinnamon mixture over top of loaves. Bake 60-70 minutes, or until firm in center. Cool, then refrigerate until ready to use. Remove loaves from pans and slice each loaf into 12 slices.

To make Orange Custard Sauce: In a medium saucepan, heat cream and milk together until just under boiling point. Remove from heat. In a medium bowl, whisk together egg yolks and sugar until light colored. Gradually add hot milk mixture to eggs. Return milk/egg mixture to pan and cook over low heat, stirring constantly, until thickened. Remove from heat and add orange syrup. Note: The custard sauce will keep for several days in refrigerator. Heat very slowly before serving.

To make French Toast: In a medium bowl, whisk together the 4 eggs and 1/2 cup half-and-half. Dip each slice in the mixture and fry in a greased skillet until golden brown on each side. Cooked slices may be kept in a 300-325°F. oven until all slices are fried. Spoon orange custard sauce onto each serving plate and place 2 slices of French toast on top.

Tudor Inn

O riginally built in 1910, the Tudor Inn Bed and Breakfast is of English Tudor design. The living room and library invite guests to relax, read or enjoy conversation. Views from the balcony include the Olympic Mountains and the Strait of Juan de Fuca. Breakfast is prepared with fresh, quality ingredients and served in the formal dining room.

Sports aficionados will enjoy cross-country skiing at nearby Hurricane Ridge.

INNKEEPERS:	*Jane Glass*
ADDRESS:	*1108 South Oak Street*
	Port Angeles, WA 98362
TELEPHONE:	*(360) 452-3138*
FAX:	*Not Available*
E-MAIL:	*tudorinfo@aol.com*
WEBSITE:	*www.northolympic.com/tudorinn*
ROOMS:	*5 Rooms; All with private baths*
OPEN:	*Year-round*
CHILDREN:	*Children over the age of 12 are welcome*
ANIMALS:	*Prohibited*
SMOKING:	*Permitted on outside porch*

Tudor Inn Apple French Toast

Makes 6-8 servings

*Caramel apple lovers will enjoy the great flavor of this French toast!
Preparation is done the night before, making morning a breeze!*

1 1/8 cups brown sugar
1/2 cup (1 stick) butter
2 tablespoons light corn syrup
2 apples, peeled and thinly sliced
1 loaf French bread, sliced 3/4-inch thick
5 eggs
1 1/2 cups milk
1 teaspoon vanilla
Maple syrup

In a medium saucepan, combine brown sugar, butter and corn syrup; cook over medium heat, stirring frequently, until mixture starts to bubble. Remove from heat and pour into 17x11-inch jelly-roll pan. Spread apple slices over syrup mixture. Place bread slices on top of apples. In a medium bowl, whisk or beat together eggs, milk and vanilla and pour (or spoon) mixture evenly over bread. Cover and refrigerate overnight.

Next morning: PREHEAT OVEN TO 350°F. Bake uncovered for 40-45 minutes, or until browned. Offer maple syrup.

The Villa

THE VILLA

Upstairs at The Villa Bed and Breakfast, guests find four unique suites, all with amenities found in the finest hotels. The Bay View Suite offers sweeping vistas of Commencement Bay and the Olympic Mountains. The Garden Suite affords a commanding view of the Sunken Garden. The Rice Bed Suite is named for its richly carved, four-poster bed.

Tucked away on the top floor, the Maid's Quarters Suite has a private verandah.

INNKEEPERS:	*Greg & Becky Anglemyer*
ADDRESS:	*705 North 5th Street*
	Tacoma, WA 98403
TELEPHONE:	*(253) 572-1157; (888) 572-1157*
FAX:	*(253) 572-1805*
E-MAIL:	*villabb@aol.com*
WEBSITE:	*www.tribnet.com/adv/bb/villa*
ROOMS:	*2 Rooms; 2 Suites; All with private baths*
OPEN:	*Year-round*
CHILDREN:	*Children 12 and over are welcome*
ANIMALS:	*Prohibited*
SMOKING:	*Prohibited*

Baked French Toast Cockaigne

Makes 4 servings

4 eggs
1 cup milk
1/2 teaspoon salt
1/2 teaspoon vanilla
1/4 cup flour
1/4 cup brown sugar
1/4 teaspoon cinnamon
1 tablespoon butter
8 to 12 slices Italian or French bread, sliced 3/4-inch thick
Cherry, blueberry or apple pie filling

PREHEAT OVEN TO 400°F. In a medium bowl, combine eggs, milk, salt and vanilla. Set aside. In a small bowl, combine (for topping) flour, brown sugar, cinnamon and butter. Mix until crumbly. Set aside. Coat 4 individual baking dishes with nonstick cooking spray. Dip bread slices into the egg/milk mixture and arrange 2 or 3 overlapping slices in each baking dish. (The number of slices used depends on the dish size as well as size of loaf.) Spread pie filling in a line across center of overlapping bread slices. Sprinkle with topping. Bake approximately 15 minutes, or until browned and crispy.

Carol's Corner

I tested this recipe using cherry pie filling. It was easy to make, colorful to serve, and tasted great! Make-ahead tip: Becky, at The Villa, suggests making your morning easier by preparing the topping ahead of time. The bread can even be dipped in the egg mixture the night before, arranged in individual baking dishes and refrigerated. She says it's best to add the toppings, however, right before baking.

The Inn at Burg's Landing

T he logo for The Inn at Burg's Landing consists of a silhouette of two majestic evergreens that were planted in 1929 by Chester and Edna Burg in celebration of their wedding day. These trees represent the steadfast commitment to the Burg family heritage of warm, friendly and personal hospitality toward all guests who share this island refuge.

Guests enjoy spectacular views of Mount Rainier, the Cascades and Puget Sound.

INNKEEPERS:	*Ken & Annie Burg*
ADDRESS:	*8808 Villa Beach Road*
	Anderson Island, WA 98303
TELEPHONE:	*(253) 884-9185; (800) 431-5622*
FAX:	*Not Available*
E-MAIL:	*innatburgslanding@mailexcite.com*
WEBSITE:	*Not Available*
ROOMS:	*4 Rooms; Private and shared baths*
OPEN:	*Year-round*
CHILDREN:	*Welcome*
ANIMALS:	*Prohibited*
SMOKING:	*Permitted on outside deck*

Baked Stuffed French Toast

Makes 5 servings (2 slices each)

By baking the French toast, it's easy to serve a group of people all at once. Annie, at The Inn at Burg's Landing, suggests serving this French toast with bacon or sausage, fresh fruit, juice, and assorted jams and syrups.

1 (8-ounce) package cream cheese, room temperature
2 tablespoons vanilla
2 tablespoons sugar
1/3 cup chopped nuts
10 slices French bread, sliced 1-inch thick
6 eggs
1/2 cup milk
1/2 teaspoon ground cinnamon
1/2 teaspoon ground nutmeg

PREHEAT OVEN TO 375°F. In a small bowl, blend cream cheese, vanilla, sugar and nuts. Set aside. With the point of a sharp knife, in each slice of bread, make a slit in the center of the top crust cutting down a couple inches to make a "pocket". Spread about 1 tablespoon of cream cheese mixture in each pocket. In a large bowl, beat together eggs, milk, cinnamon and nutmeg. Dip each slice of bread into egg mixture, soaking thoroughly. Put slices onto a greased baking sheet and bake for about 20 minutes, or until lightly browned.

Northern Lights

Located on the majestic Columbia River, eight miles south of the Canadian border, the Northern Lights Bed and Breakfast provides a pleasant relief from urban hassles. With turn-of-the-century grandeur, this completely remodeled and beautifully decorated home is filled with comfort and warm hospitality.

With five distinct seasons (including Indian summer), sports activities abound.

INNKEEPERS:	*Sam & Angelia Davis*
ADDRESS:	*3383 Lot 10, Hwy 25 N*
	Northport, WA 99157
TELEPHONE:	*(509) 732-4345*
FAX:	*(509) 732-4586*
E-MAIL:	*davisent@triax.com*
WEBSITE:	*Not Available*
ROOMS:	*6 Rooms; Private and shared baths*
OPEN:	*Year-round*
CHILDREN:	*Children eight and older are welcome*
ANIMALS:	*Prohibited*
SMOKING:	*Permitted outside only*

Apple Breakfast Lasagna

Makes 6 large servings

1 cup sour cream
1/3 cup brown sugar
2 (12-ounce) packages frozen French toast
8 ounces sliced boiled ham (12 slices)
1 (8-ounce) package (2 cups) Sargento 3 Cheese Gourmet Cheddar,
    divided
1 (20-ounce) can apple pie filling
1 cup granola

PREHEAT OVEN TO 350°F. In a small bowl, blend sour cream and brown sugar. Chill. Place 6 French toast slices in bottom of greased 13x9-inch baking dish. Layer ham, 1 1/2 cups cheese and remaining 6 slices of French toast. Spread apple pie filling over the top and sprinkle with granola. Bake for 25 minutes. Top with remaining 1/2 cup cheese and bake 5 minutes longer or until cheese is melted. Serve with sour cream and brown sugar mixture.

Island Escape

Guests of the Island Escape Bed and Breakfast enjoy a luxurious first floor suite furnished with a beautifully carved German hutch, Cal-King bed and private Jacuzzi bath. Innkeeper Paula offers additional amenities in the popular "Honeymoon Package."

"We came for one night and stayed for four. This is the finest place we've ever stayed."

~ Guest, Island Escape

INNKEEPERS:	*Paula E. Pascoe*
ADDRESS:	*210 Island Blvd.*
	Fox Island, WA 98333
TELEPHONE:	*(253) 549-2044*
FAX:	*Not Available*
E-MAIL:	*islandescape@narrows.com*
WEBSITE:	*www.narrows.com/islandescape*
ROOMS:	*1 Executive Suite; Private bath*
OPEN:	*Year-round*
CHILDREN:	*Welcome*
ANIMALS:	*Prohibited*
SMOKING:	*Prohibited*

Island Escape's House Granola

Makes about 8 cups

4 cups rolled oats
1/4 cup unrefined safflower oil
1/4 cup honey
1 1/2 teaspoons vanilla
1/2 cup sesame seeds
1/2 cup chopped almonds, unsalted
1/2 cup chopped cashews, unsalted
1 cup raisins
Optional variations: For a distinctive "island" touch, add coconut
    and dried unsweetened pineapple.
    Or use your favorite dried fruits, such as apricots, apples, banana
    chips and cranberries.

PREHEAT OVEN TO 350°F. Using a very large cookie sheet or large shallow baking pan, toast rolled oats in oven for 15 minutes, stirring once or twice to ensure even baking. In a small saucepan, combine oil, honey and vanilla and heat until warm. Set aside. In a large bowl, mix together sesame seeds, almonds and cashews. Pour the warm oil/honey mixture over seeds and nuts. Stir to combine and then pour combined mixture over the oats. Blend well. Bake for about 20 minutes, turning oats every five minutes. Watch carefully so it doesn't get too brown. (Set the timer to insure a nice uniform golden brown granola.) Add raisins and any other optional ingredients when done cooking.

"Credit for this recipe goes to Kim, my husband's daughter. She was a blue ribbon graduate of Peter Kump's New York Cooking School and she is currently a Pastry Assistant at The Coyote Café in Santa Fe. Several of Kim's recipes are incorporated in our menus at Island Escape B & B. We serve this House Granola with our bowl of hot Montana whole-wheat cereal. It is the main entrée and is presented with juice, coffee or tea, in season fresh fruit plate and homemade muffins or a quick bread."

Paula Pascoe - Island Escape

Petersen

... *Welcome*...

Originally built in the 1940's, the Petersen Bed and Breakfast has been renovated several times and now includes a spa on the deck. After a restful night's sleep, guests delight in a savory home-style breakfast that is served in the atrium kitchen.

"Make our home your Bellevue home."

~ Owners, Petersen B & B

INNKEEPERS:	*Eunice & Carl Petersen*
ADDRESS:	*10228 S.E. 8th*
	Bellevue, WA 98004
TELEPHONE:	*(425) 454-9334*
FAX:	*Not Available*
E-MAIL:	*nuna@sttl.uswest.net*
WEBSITE:	*Not Available*
ROOMS:	*2 Rooms; Shared baths*
OPEN:	*Year-round*
CHILDREN:	*Welcome*
ANIMALS:	*Prohibited*
SMOKING:	*Permitted on outside deck*

Eunice's Yummy Granola

Makes about 8 cups

4 cups rolled oats
1 cup oat bran or wheat germ
1/4 cup sesame seeds, raw
1/4 cup flax seeds
1/4 cup sunflower seeds, raw, unsalted
1/2 cup or more coarsely chopped almonds or other nuts
1 cup canola oil
3/4 cup honey
3/4 teaspoon salt
1 teaspoon vanilla
1/4 teaspoon almond extract
1/4 teaspoon maple flavoring
1 cup natural shredded coconut

PREHEAT OVEN TO 350°F. In a large baking dish, combine oats, bran or wheat germ, sesame seeds, flax seeds, sunflower seeds and nuts. Set aside. In a medium saucepan, heat together oil, honey, salt, and flavorings. Pour warm mixture over dry ingredients, stirring until well combined. Place in oven and toast for 30 minutes, stirring once or twice during baking. Lower oven heat to 325°F. and continue baking, stirring every 5 minutes, until browned to your liking. <u>Watch carefully</u> so granola does not burn. Add coconut when granola is cooked and hot out of oven. Cool completely and store in an airtight container.

> **Carol's Corner**
>
> *Granola freezes well, so bake up a big batch and enjoy!*

The James House

S itting high on a bluff overlooking Port Townsend Bay, The James House is a grand Victorian mansion with sweeping views of the Cascade and Olympic mountain ranges. On the National Register of Historic Places, this old mansion is a reminder of a bygone era when the bay was filled with sailing ships.

The James House was the first bed and breakfast in the Pacific Northwest.

INNKEEPERS: *Carol McGough*
ADDRESS: *1238 Washington Street*
Port Townsend, WA 98368
TELEPHONE: *(360) 385-1238; (800) 385-1238*
FAX: *(360) 379-5551*
E-MAIL: *carolmcg@olympus.net*
WEBSITE: *www.jameshouse.com*
ROOMS: *8 Rooms; 4 Suites; 1 Cottage; All with private*
OPEN: *baths*
Year-round
CHILDREN: *Children 12 and older are welcome*
ANIMALS: *Prohibited*
SMOKING: *Prohibited*

Fruit and Yogurt Bircher Muesli

Makes 12 servings

2 cups rolled oats
Milk, to cover oats
3/4 cup seedless red grapes
1 cup pineapple, diced (fresh or canned)
2 pears, diced (fresh or canned)
1/2 banana, halved and sliced
16 ounces peach yogurt
1/3 cup honey
2 sweet apples
Toasted coconut (directions below)

Place uncooked oats in a medium bowl and just cover with milk. Let stand for 15 minutes. Meanwhile, in a large bowl, toss together grapes, pineapple, pears and banana. Stir in the yogurt. Set aside. Add honey to oats, mixing well. Grate apples (peeled or unpeeled) and mix into oats. Add oat/apple mixture to fruit/yogurt mixture. Serve 1/2-cup portions in individual bowls and top each with 1 tablespoon toasted coconut.

To toast coconut: PREHEAT OVEN TO 350°F. Spread shredded coconut in a single layer on a cookie sheet or in a shallow baking pan. Bake approximately 10 minutes, stirring occasionally, until coconut is evenly browned and lightly toasted. Cool completely and store in airtight container.

> **Carol's Corner**
>
> *The German word* muesli *means mixture. Muesli was developed as a health food near the end of the 19th century by a Swiss nutritionist named Dr. Bircher-Benner. Muesli is a delicious and healthful way to start the day!*

Mimi's Cottage by the Sea

M imi's Cottage by the Sea is located on Vashon Island in Puget Sound. Surrounded by a hillside garden, this private cottage offers a completely furnished kitchen, wood stove fireplace and a breathtaking view of Mount Rainier.

Innkeeper Gloria wanted her grandchildren to call her Mimi. When they didn't, she gave her cottage this pet name. As a result, many guests call her Mimi.

INNKEEPERS:	*Gloria Olson*
ADDRESS:	*7923 S.W. Hawthorne Lane*
	Vashon Island, WA 98070
TELEPHONE:	*(206) 567-4383*
FAX:	*(206) 567-4383 (Call ahead)*
E-MAIL:	*Not Available*
WEBSITE:	*Not Available*
ROOMS:	*2 Rooms; 1 Cottage; All with private baths*
OPEN:	*Year-round*
CHILDREN:	*Prohibited*
ANIMALS:	*Prohibited*
SMOKING:	*Prohibited*

Baked Oatmeal à la Becky

Makes 3-4 servings

Serve this delicious morning treat with cream or half-and-half, chopped nuts, yogurt, brown sugar or whatever sounds good. Enjoy!

1 1/2 cups old-fashioned rolled oats (do not use the "quick" variety)
2 tablespoons brown sugar
Cinnamon to taste
Raisins
Dried fruit pieces
1 or 2 fresh apples or pears, peeled and cubed
2 cups warm milk

PREHEAT OVEN TO 350°F. In an ovenproof dish, mix together oats, brown sugar, cinnamon, raisins and dried fruit. Add fresh fruit and warm milk. Stir to combine. Bake uncovered for 25 minutes.

Carol's Corner

This easy oatmeal recipe, loaded with fruit, received rave reviews from visiting relatives Brian, Linda, Quinn, Dylan and Janet. I enjoyed having their input for several days in the taste-testing process for this book.

Lizzie's

J ust beyond the front door of Lizzie's Bed and Breakfast, guests discover the gracious service and unhurried atmosphere of a gentler era. Original wallpaper from 1888 adorns the walls. A delectable breakfast is served in the sunny kitchen at the great oak table.

Decorated in pale amber hues and golden woods, Daisy's Room harbors a secret. Hidden on the wall is Daisy's delicate signature, dated February 25, 1894.

INNKEEPERS:	*Bill & Patti Wickline*
ADDRESS:	*731 Pierce Street*
	Port Townsend, WA 98368
TELEPHONE:	*(360) 385-4168; (800) 700-4168*
FAX:	*(360) 385-9467*
E-MAIL:	*wickline@olympus.net*
WEBSITE:	*www.kolke.com/lizzies*
ROOMS:	*7 Rooms; All with private baths*
OPEN:	*Year-round*
CHILDREN:	*Children over the age of 10 are welcome*
ANIMALS:	*Prohibited*
SMOKING:	*Prohibited*

Patti's Porridge

Makes 6-8 servings

Quick-cooking oatmeal
Water
Salt
4 tablespoons (1/2 stick) margarine
3/4 cup brown sugar
1 tablespoon cinnamon (or less to taste)
2 or 3 bananas, sliced

Prepare oatmeal for 6-8 people according to package directions. To make the sauce, in a medium sauté pan, melt margarine and stir in brown sugar and cinnamon until combined. Stir just until it starts bubbling around edges, then remove from heat. Stir in bananas. Put oatmeal in a large serving bowl (or individual bowls) and pour banana sauce over top of oatmeal.

"The topping to this oatmeal will convert the most skeptic of oatmeal eaters! Serve with a pitcher of milk for those who must have it."

Patti Wickline - Lizzie's Victorian Bed & Breakfast

Egg Entrées

Egg Entrées

S crumptious, three-course breakfasts await guests of the Baker House Bed and Breakfast. Located three blocks from the waterfront, this historic inn affords gorgeous views of Port Townsend Bay.

"This is what a B & B should be like."

~ Guest, Baker House B & B

INNKEEPERS:	*Herb & Jean Herrington*
ADDRESS:	*905 Franklin*
	Port Townsend, WA 98368
TELEPHONE:	*(360) 385-6673*
FAX:	*(360) 385-6673 (Call ahead)*
E-MAIL:	*Not Available*
WEBSITE:	*Not Available*
ROOMS:	*4 Rooms; Private and shared baths*
OPEN:	*Year-round*
CHILDREN:	*Children 14 and older are welcome*
ANIMALS:	*Prohibited*
SMOKING:	*Prohibited*

Herb's Special Breakfast

Makes 2-4 servings, depending on size of appetites

1 tablespoon oil
2 cups onion (Herb likes even up to 3 cups)
1 or 2 cloves garlic, minced
1/2 pound lean ground beef
Salt, to taste
Pepper, to taste
Oregano, to taste
1 (8-ounce) can sliced mushrooms, drained
1/3 of (10-ounce) package frozen chopped spinach, thawed
4 eggs, well beaten
1/4 cup Parmesan cheese

Heat oil in a large sauté pan. Cook onions until they just start to get tender. Add garlic and sauté a few minutes more. Stir in beef and cook until meat is done but still a little pink in places. Season with salt, pepper and oregano. Drain off fat, if any. Note: At this point the pan may be covered and set aside as you prepare the rest of your meal.

<u>To finish the dish</u>: Squeeze out moisture from spinach. Add the spinach and mushrooms to the meat mixture and heat. Check seasonings and remedy if needed. Add the eggs. Mix until eggs are fully cooked (mixture will be fairly dry). Serve on warmed plates and sprinkle with Parmesan cheese.

<u>Serving suggestion</u>: Toasted bread and sliced fresh fruit go well with this dish.

"You can modify this recipe to be a light dinner meal. Instead of the ground beef, substitute any combination of shelled shrimp, scallops and white fish, only add them just before the eggs so they don't get overcooked."

Herb Herrington - Baker House

Log Castle

Located on Whidbey Island, the Log Castle Bed and Breakfast is a charming lodge that provides gracious accommodations to all who wish to experience the peace and quiet of island life. Guests are delighted by magnificent views of Mount Baker and the beautiful Cascade Mountains.

Homemade breads, muffins and cinnamon rolls may be included in the three-course breakfast that is served family-style on the log table.

INNKEEPERS:	*Karen & Phil Holdsworth*
	Owners: Jack & Norma Metcalf
ADDRESS:	*4693 Saratoga Road*
	Langley, WA 98260
TELEPHONE:	*(360) 221-5483*
FAX:	*(360) 221-6249*
E-MAIL:	*innkeepr@whidbey.com*
WEBSITE:	*www.whidbey.com/logcastle*
ROOMS:	*4 Rooms; All with private baths*
OPEN:	*Year-round*
CHILDREN:	*Children 10 and older are welcome*
ANIMALS:	*Prohibited*
SMOKING:	*Prohibited*

Log Castle Eggs on the Half Shell

Makes 1 serving (increase as needed)

Seashell
1/2 cup shredded Swiss cheese (or pepper jack)
1 egg
1 tablespoon half-and-half
Cooked bacon
Black pepper, to taste

PREHEAT OVEN TO 350°F. Coat seashell liberally with nonstick cooking spray. Make "nest" of cheese in seashell (reserve a small amount of cheese to sprinkle on top, or use some additional cheese). Break egg into "nest". Pour half-and-half over yolk. Crumble bacon over egg and shake on black pepper. Sprinkle with remaining cheese. Bake for about 15 minutes or longer until egg is done to your liking.

Carol's Corner

A handy tip I learned from my mother is to cook a whole package of bacon at one time and freeze the cooked slices. Then whenever you want a few slices of bacon for anything, just remove the amount needed from the freezer and heat it in the microwave for a few seconds until heated through. It tastes just like fresh-cooked bacon! For the above recipe, you wouldn't even need to heat the bacon. Just take a slice from the freezer and crumble it on top of the egg! Easy!

Mill Town Manor

Originally built in 1925 by lumber baron T.S. Galbraith, the Mill Town Bed and Breakfast is a National Historic Register Landmark. This 6,000-square-foot estate celebrates the flamboyant elegance of the "Roaring 20's." Guests delight in the secret passageway to the Prohibition Era speakeasy that is complete with bar and dance floor.

The Gatsby Room features a raised queen-sized bed with a draped canopy headboard.

INNKEEPERS: *Gary & Debbi Saint*
ADDRESS: *116 Oak Street*
Eatonville, WA 98328
TELEPHONE: *(360) 832-6506*
FAX: *(360) 832-6506*
E-MAIL: *milltown@foxinternet.net*
WEBSITE: *www.bbonline.com/wa/milltown/*
ROOMS: *5 Rooms; All with private baths*
OPEN: *Year-round*
CHILDREN: *Children six and older are welcome*
ANIMALS: *Prohibited*
SMOKING: *Prohibited*

Northwest Eggs Benedict

Makes 4-6 servings

8 eggs, hard-boiled and sliced
8 stalks fresh asparagus, steamed until tender
(or canned)
2 to 4 ounces smoked salmon, flaked

<u>Sauce</u>

3/4 cup (1 1/2 sticks) butter or margarine
3/4 cup flour
6 cups milk
1 1/2 cups cheddar cheese, shredded (optional)
Salt, to taste
Pepper, to taste
Paprika, for garnish
Biscuits, cornbread or thick slices of toast (accompaniments)

PREHEAT OVEN TO 350°F. Coat 4 (16-ounce) custard cups or individual casserole dishes (for large servings), or 6 (12-ounce) cups (for smaller servings), with nonstick cooking spray. Divide egg slices equally among the dishes, followed by asparagus spears. (If you wish, cut asparagus into bite-size pieces to make eating easier.) Sprinkle with flaked salmon. <u>To prepare the sauce</u>: Melt butter in a medium saucepan over moderate heat. Blend in flour. Add milk gradually, stirring constantly (a wire whisk works well) until thick and smooth. Add cheese and stir until melted. Season to taste with salt and pepper. Pour sauce into each individual dish and sprinkle with paprika. Bake for 25-30 minutes, or until heated and bubbly. Serve with biscuits, cornbread or toast.

Olympic Lights

O verlooking the panorama of the Pacific Ocean and the Olympic Mountain Range, the Olympic Lights Bed and Breakfast sits in an open meadow on San Juan Island. Guests of this wondrous guest home recapture simple pleasures by walking through open meadows and strolling the spectacular beaches of American Camp.

A full breakfast includes eggs from the resident hens.

INNKEEPERS:	*Christian & Lea Androde*
ADDRESS:	*4531- A Cattle Point Road*
	Friday Harbor, WA 98250
TELEPHONE:	*(360) 378-3186*
FAX:	*(360) 378-2097*
E-MAIL:	*Not Available*
WEBSITE:	*www.sanjuaninfo.com*
ROOMS:	*5 Rooms; Private and shared baths*
OPEN:	*Year-round*
CHILDREN:	*Children 10 and older are welcome*
ANIMALS:	*Prohibited*
SMOKING:	*Prohibited*

Eggs with Potato and Red Pepper-Onion Sauce

Makes 6 servings

Make the Red Pepper-Onion Sauce ahead of time. Freeze in small one-cup portions and you'll be ready to make this egg dish almost any time. This recipe is great for when you have leftover potatoes.

Olive oil or butter, for sautéing
1 cup chopped sweet onion
2 cups cubed (1/4-inch) cooked potato
1 cup Red Pepper-Onion Sauce (recipe below)
12 eggs
2 tablespoons cottage cheese
3/4 cup shredded cheddar cheese

First, make the Red Pepper-Onion Sauce (recipe below), then proceed with the following directions. PREHEAT BROILER. Place olive oil (or butter) in medium sauté pan and cook onion until tender. Add potato and one cup of Red Pepper-Onion Sauce. Heat gently and set aside; cover with foil to keep warm. In a large bowl, beat eggs. In a large nonstick pan, coated with cooking spray (or butter), cook eggs over very low heat. Just as eggs begin to set, add cottage cheese. Remove from heat (eggs should be very moist). Coat 6 individual baking dishes with nonstick cooking spray. Spoon eggs into dishes and top with potato/red pepper/onion mixture. Sprinkle each dish with 2 tablespoons cheddar cheese. Broil about 3 minutes and serve.

Red Pepper-Onion Sauce

Makes 6 cups

8 to 10 red peppers
3 large sweet white onions, chopped
Olive oil or butter, for sautéing
Salt, to taste

PREHEAT BROILER. Cut peppers in half lengthwise; discard seeds and stems. Place skin-side up on foil-covered cookie sheet. Roast red peppers under broiler for 10 minutes or longer, until charred. Cool peppers in a brown paper bag, about 15 minutes. Peel off skin. Sauté chopped onions in olive oil or butter until caramelized. Purée onions and peppers in food processor or blender. Add salt, if desired. Freeze extra sauce for later use.

Carol's Corner

This is a great breakfast dish! And a perfect one for vegetarians! For a nice color contrast, garnish each dish with a touch of sour cream and a fresh parsley sprig.

Soundview

Located 100 feet above Puget Sound, the Soundview Bed and Breakfast is a solitary guest house that overlooks the shipping lanes between Seattle and Tacoma. This private suite includes a kitchen, dining area, living room and bedroom with king-sized bed. A delectable breakfast is served after a peaceful night's rest.

From the deck, guests enjoy glorious sunsets while observing the resident eagles.

INNKEEPERS:	*Gerry & Dick Flaten*
ADDRESS:	*17600 Sylvester Rd SW*
	Seattle, WA 98166
TELEPHONE:	*(206) 244-5209; (888) 244-5209*
FAX:	*(206) 243-8687*
E-MAIL:	*soundview@sprynet.com*
WEBSITE:	*www.eskimo.com/~cyclone/sv.html*
ROOMS:	*1 Cottage; Private bath*
OPEN:	*Year-round*
CHILDREN:	*Prohibited*
ANIMALS:	*Prohibited*
SMOKING:	*Prohibited*

Baked Egg and Potato Puff

Makes 2 servings

4 eggs
2 teaspoons water
1/4 cup shredded cheddar cheese
8 mini Tater Tots (or use 4 regular size and cut in half)

PREHEAT OVEN TO 350°F. Coat two (1 cup) ramekins with nonstick cooking spray. In a medium bowl, beat together eggs and water. Add cheese and potatoes. Stir to combine. Divide between two ramekins. Bake uncovered for 20-25 minutes. Puffs up like a soufflé. Serve immediately.

Make-ahead tip: After baking, these can be cooled, covered with plastic wrap and refrigerated. Reheat in microwave.

Carol's Corner

I tried this recipe using a 3/4-cup ramekin. The uncooked egg mixture filled the dish to the very top. After 25 minutes of baking, the egg and potato had puffed up to 1 1/2-inches above the rim of the dish. It looked great to serve! I suggest offering ketchup or salsa for those who like the extra flavor.

Stratford Manor

T he Stratford Manor Bed and Breakfast is situated on 30 acres with panoramic views of the Pacific Northwest countryside. The rooms offer a romantic escape with their cozy comforters, sitting areas, gas fireplaces and Jacuzzi tubs.

"Thanks for the pampering."

~ Guest, Stratford Manor

INNKEEPERS:	*Leslie & Jim Lohse*
ADDRESS:	*1416 Van Wyck Road*
	Bellingham, WA 98226
TELEPHONE:	*(360) 715-8441*
FAX:	*(360) 671-0840*
E-MAIL:	*llohse@aol.com*
WEBSITE:	*www.site-works.com/stratford*
ROOMS:	*3 Rooms; All with private baths*
OPEN:	*Year-round*
CHILDREN:	*Prohibited*
ANIMALS:	*Prohibited*
SMOKING:	*Permitted on outside porch*

Veggie Benedict

Makes 4 servings

A colorful medley of vegetables teamed with poached eggs.

1 to 2 tablespoons olive oil
4 raw potatoes diced (peeled or unpeeled)
Salt, to taste
Pepper, to taste
Dried, crushed basil leaves, to taste
1/2 green pepper, thinly sliced
1/2 red or orange pepper, thinly sliced
1/2 yellow pepper, thinly sliced
3/4 cup sliced mushrooms
3 green onions, sliced
Hollandaise sauce (your favorite recipe or use Knorr's mix)
4 eggs, poached
Optional garnishes: Paprika, parsley, fresh fruit,
    edible flowers

Heat olive oil in a large sauté pan over medium heat. Add potatoes and season with salt, pepper and basil; cook for approximately 20 minutes. Add remaining vegetables and sauté until "tender crisp" (vegetables will be tender, but still have a "bite" to them). While vegetables are cooking, prepare Hollandaise sauce and cook eggs.

To serve: Divide vegetables between four plates. Place a poached egg on each and top with sauce. Garnish with paprika and parsley and, if desired, decorate each plate with fresh fruit and flowers.

Chestnut Hill Inn

E ach room at the Chestnut Hill Inn Bed and Breakfast on Orcas Island is unique and contains the amenities expected by the discriminating traveler. Elegant queen-sized beds, piled high with luxurious pillows and soft down comforters, create the feeling of sleeping on a cloud.

Cozy rooms and candlelight dinners set the tone for the "romantic at heart".

INNKEEPERS:	*Daniel & Marilyn Loewke*
ADDRESS:	*PO Box 213*
	Orcas, WA 98280
TELEPHONE:	*(360) 376-5157*
FAX:	*(360) 376-5283*
E-MAIL:	*chestnut@pacificrim.net*
WEBSITE:	*www.chestnuthillinn.com*
ROOMS:	*4 Rooms; 1 Suite; 1 Cottage; All with*
	private baths
OPEN:	*Year-round*
CHILDREN:	*Children 13 and older are welcome*
	(Call ahead)
ANIMALS:	*Prohibited*
SMOKING:	*Prohibited*

Rolled Smoked Ham, Spinach and Gruyère Omelet

Makes 4 servings

For a colorful presentation, serve with a slice of cantaloupe and several bright red strawberries. A bagel or muffin completes the meal.

1/2 cup flour
1 cup milk
2 tablespoons butter, melted
1/2 teaspoon salt
4 eggs
1 cup chopped fully cooked smoked ham
1 small onion (or 1 leek, or 5 green onions), chopped
1 1/2 cups shredded Gruyère or Swiss cheese
1 cup chopped fresh spinach leaves
4 large, whole spinach leaves, for serving

PREHEAT OVEN TO 350°F. Line a 15x10-inch jelly-roll pan with aluminum foil, making sure the foil goes all the way up all four sides of pan. Generously coat foil with nonstick cooking spray. (Do not use butter as it will burn and egg mixture will stick.) Using food processor, blend together flour, milk, butter, salt and eggs. Pour into prepared pan. Sprinkle evenly with ham and onions. Bake until eggs are set, about 15-18 minutes. Remove from oven and immediately sprinkle with cheese and spinach. Beginning at narrow end of the omelet, roll up, using foil to help lift and roll omelet.

<u>To serve</u>: Arrange one whole spinach leaf on each serving plate. Cut rolled omelet into 8 slices (each approximately 1 1/4-inch thick) and place two slices on each plate on top of spinach leaf.

"You can substitute anything in this easy recipe, and what a way to do omelets. No fuss, no mess!"

Marilyn Loewke - Chestnut Hill Inn

The Compass Rose

P. INKLSK

T he Compass Rose Bed and Breakfast on Whidbey Island,
Washington, is idyllically situated in Coupeville, the heart of Ebey's
Landing Historical Reserve. This elegant 1890's Queen Anne Victorian
home is furnished with glorious antiques.

After arrival, guests enjoy afternoon tea. A sumptuous breakfast is
presented on exquisite china, crystal, silver, linen and lace.

INNKEEPERS:	*Captain & Mrs. Marshall Bronson*
ADDRESS:	*508 South Main Street*
	Coupeville, WA 98239
TELEPHONE:	*(360) 678-5318; (800) 237-3881*
FAX:	*(360) 678-5318*
E-MAIL:	*Not Available*
WEBSITE:	*www.whidbey.net/compassrose*
ROOMS:	*2 Rooms; Private and shared baths*
OPEN:	*Year-round*
CHILDREN:	*Well-behaved children are welcome*
ANIMALS:	*Prohibited*
SMOKING:	*Prohibited*

Wild Rice Omelets

Makes 4 omelets

4 eggs
2 tablespoons cream
1/2 teaspoon dried chervil (or parsley)
1/4 teaspoon salt
1/4 teaspoon pepper
1 tablespoon + 4 teaspoons butter, divided
1 small onion, chopped
1/2 red pepper, chopped
1/2 green pepper, chopped
1/2 yellow pepper, chopped
1 teaspoon Herbes de Provence (or Italian seasoning)
1 cup cooked wild rice (cooked in chicken stock or bouillon)
Parsley, fresh herbs, and nasturtium flowers, for garnish

In a medium bowl, beat together eggs, cream, chervil, salt and pepper until frothy. In a medium frying pan, melt one tablespoon butter and sauté onions until translucent. Add all three kinds of peppers and Herbes de Provence and sauté until peppers are "tender crisp" (peppers will be tender, but still have a "bite" to them). On the stovetop in a 6-inch cast iron skillet (or other ovenproof pan), melt one teaspoon butter. Add 1/4 of the egg mixture. Over the eggs, sprinkle 1/4 of the wild rice and 1/4 of the sautéed vegetables. Cook over medium-low heat for 1 minute, then place under broiler (2nd shelf or about 7-inches down) about 2 minutes until eggs set and begin to rise. Remove to warm plate and repeat to make 3 more omelets. Garnish with parsley, fresh herbs, and nasturtium flowers.

🌿 Carol's Corner

There is a great spice and tea shop in Seattle located in Pike Place Market called MarketSpice. They sell items in bulk so you can buy small amounts of spices and herbs that you don't use often (like Herbes de Provence and chervil used in the above recipe), thus saving money. In addition to their spices and teas, they have a variety of salt-free seasonings and regular and flavored coffees. If you are in the area, be sure to stop in — you'll enjoy the experience!

Bellingham's DeCann House

L ocated in a university town, Bellingham's DeCann House Bed and Breakfast overlooks Bellingham Bay and the San Juan Islands. Innkeepers Van and Barbara are life-long Northwest residents who have restored this grand old home.

Barbara is a glass hobbyist who has ornamented the house with stained glass and etchings. Van, a jack-of-all-trades, has renovated seven older homes.

INNKEEPERS:	*Barbara and Van Hudson*
ADDRESS:	*2610 Eldridge Avenue*
	Bellingham, WA 98225
TELEPHONE:	*(360) 734-9172*
FAX:	*Not Available*
E-MAIL:	*hudson@pacificrim.net*
WEBSITE:	*www.pacificrim.net/~hudson*
ROOMS:	*2 Rooms; Private baths*
OPEN:	*Thanksgiving through December*
CHILDREN:	*Children over the age of 12 are welcome*
ANIMALS:	*Prohibited*
SMOKING:	*Permitted outside on covered porches*

DeCann House Omelet

Makes 2 servings (double or triple as needed)

Quick, easy and yummy!

2 tablespoons butter
1 green onion, sliced
2 cups frozen hash browns
Salt, to taste
Pepper, to taste
2 eggs
1 tablespoon milk
2 strips bacon, cooked and crumbled
3/4 cup grated cheddar cheese
2 tablespoons cream cheese, cubed

In a 9-inch glass pie plate (or other microwave-safe dish), cook butter and onion in microwave oven for 30 seconds. Add potatoes, salt and pepper. Microwave on high for 2 minutes. Stir and cook for 2 more minutes. In a small bowl, lightly beat eggs and milk. Pour over cooked potatoes. Add cooked bacon; stir. Sprinkle grated cheese (save a bit of grated cheese for garnish) and cubed cheese on top of eggs and potatoes. Cook for 2 minutes. Check edges to see if more time is needed. Eggs should be moist but not runny. Be careful not to overcook. If more time is needed, cook on medium for another minute and check often. Put remaining cheese on top just before serving. We usually complement with juice and toast with homemade jam.

"This microwave dish has become Van's favorite breakfast to cook and serve, mainly because it is the kind of 'fill 'em up' breakfast he likes to eat. The trick is to experiment with the amount and type of cheese until you get the taste you like."

Barb Hudson - Bellingham's DeCann House

A Touch of Europe

A Touch of Europe Bed and Breakfast Inn is a Queen Anne Victorian that is designated on the National Register of Historic Places. Guests awaken to an appetizing European breakfast that is served in the Victorian dining room or privately in the turret.

Special arrangements can be made for gourmet picnic basket lunches, elegant four to seven course dinners or catering for weddings, meetings or other special events.

INNKEEPERS:	*Erika G. & James A. Cenci*
ADDRESS:	*220 North 16th Avenue*
	Yakima, WA 98902
TELEPHONE:	*(509) 454-9775; (888) 438-7073*
FAX:	*Not Available*
E-MAIL:	*Not Available*
WEBSITE:	*www.winesnw.com/toucheuropeb&b.htm*
ROOMS:	*3 Rooms; All with private baths*
OPEN:	*Year-round*
CHILDREN:	*Prohibited*
ANIMALS:	*Prohibited*
SMOKING:	*Permitted outside only*

Signature Brie-Chives Omelet

Makes 1 omelet

2 eggs
1 teaspoon cold water
1/2 tablespoon unsalted butter
1/2 tablespoon chopped chives
1 ounce Brie cheese, cut into 1/4-inch cubes
Suggested garnishes: fresh fruit or tomato slices

In a small bowl, lightly beat together eggs and water. Heat butter in a hot frying pan (skillet). Pour in eggs and scatter the chives and Brie evenly over whole surface. Make omelet swiftly, lifting cooked edges with a spatula and allowing uncooked portion of eggs to run underneath. Fold over and turn out onto a warm plate. Garnish with fresh fruit or tomato slices.

Carol's Corner

A melt-in-your-mouth omelet! This recipe is easy to do, yet has an elegant appeal. For extra garnish, slide two long chive pieces partway under the omelet.

Domaine Madeleine

E clectic European menus are legendary at Domaine Madeleine Bed and Breakfast. Artistic arrays of fruit, fresh-baked petite baguettes and croissants are served each morning with an assortment of exotic cheeses and jams. Appetizing breakfast entrées follow, with a light dessert being the final course of the morning meal.

The five romantic guest rooms feature fireplaces and two-person whirlpools.

INNKEEPERS:	*Madeleine & John Chambers*
ADDRESS:	*146 Wildflower Lane*
	Port Angeles, WA 98362
TELEPHONE:	*(360) 457-4174*
FAX:	*(360) 457-3037*
E-MAIL:	*domm@olypen.com*
WEBSITE:	*www.northolympic.com/dm*
ROOMS:	*1 Room; 3 Suites; 1 Cottage; All with*
	private baths
OPEN:	*Year-round*
CHILDREN:	*Children over the age of 12 are welcome*
ANIMALS:	*Prohibited*
SMOKING:	*Permitted outdoors only*

Madeleine's Ratatouille Omelet

Makes 1 large omelet (serves 2)

Plan ahead for this recipe. To make this flavorful omelet, you must first make Madeleine's wonderful ratatouille that is found on page 193.

2 tablespoons olive oil
4 eggs (or 3 whole eggs + 2 egg whites), beaten
4 tablespoons ratatouille (recipe on page 193), warmed
1 tablespoon grated Emmentaler Swiss cheese
1 tablespoon grated Vermont sharp cheddar cheese

Heat a skillet and add oil. Pour in beaten eggs. When eggs are firm, but not dry, spoon ratatouille over eggs. Fold omelet and sprinkle both kinds of grated cheese over top. Cut in half to serve.

Arbutus Lodge

Arbutus Lodge

L ocated on the "serene" side of the San Juan Islands, guests of the Arbutus Lodge enjoy peace and tranquillity as they stroll through sunny meadows and stately madronas. This delightful island retreat features two beautiful guest rooms.

Gourmet breakfasts highlight weekday mornings, while Sunday mornings feature delectable international-style specialties.

INNKEEPERS:	*Susan Argento-Millington & Richard Millington*
ADDRESS:	*1827 Westside Road North*
	Friday Harbor, WA 98250
TELEPHONE:	*(360) 378-8840*
FAX:	*Not Available*
E-MAIL:	*arbutus@rockisland.com*
WEBSITE:	*www.friday-harbor.net/arbutus*
ROOMS:	*2 Rooms; Private baths*
OPEN:	*Year-round*
CHILDREN:	*Children 12 and older are welcome*
ANIMALS:	*Prohibited*
SMOKING:	*Prohibited*

Vegetable Frittata

Makes 8 servings

A very versatile dish!

1/2 cup uncooked rice (or use 3/4 cup leftover cooked rice)
3/4 teaspoon salt, divided
3 leeks, split, rinsed and sliced crosswise
1 (10-ounce) package frozen chopped spinach, thawed and
   squeezed dry
2 zucchini, halved lengthwise, sliced crosswise
2 large carrots, grated
3 large cloves garlic, minced
2 ounces feta cheese, crumbled
3 tablespoons grated Parmesan cheese, divided
1/4 teaspoon salt
3 large whole eggs
9 egg whites
2 tablespoons chopped fresh mint
3/4 teaspoon black pepper
2 plum tomatoes, sliced

In a small saucepan, cook rice as directed on package, using 1/2 teaspoon salt and no butter. PREHEAT BROILER. Coat a large nonstick skillet with nonstick cooking spray. Over medium heat, cook leeks, covered, for 5 minutes. Add spinach, zucchini, carrots and garlic. Sauté for 3 minutes. Remove vegetables to a bowl. Stir in cooked rice, feta cheese, 2 tablespoons of Parmesan cheese and 1/4 teaspoon salt. Set aside. In a medium bowl, whisk or beat whole eggs, egg whites, mint and pepper. Coat a large ovenproof skillet with nonstick cooking spray. Over medium-high heat, add vegetable mixture, spreading evenly, and pour in egg mixture. Cook 2 minutes, lifting at edges. Cover and cook 3 minutes. Place skillet 3-4-inches under broiler, for 5 minutes, or until brown. Arrange tomato slices on top and sprinkle with remaining Parmesan cheese. Broil to melt cheese.

Old Consulate Inn
(F.W. Hastings House)

S itting high on a bluff with commanding views of Port Townsend Bay, Mount Rainier and the Olympic Mountains, the Old Consulate Inn is Port Townsend's founding family mansion. Originally built in 1889 by Senator F.W. Hastings, this grand mansion has become one of the most photographed and artistically depicted Victorians in the Pacific Northwest.

The Old Consulate Inn is a designated National Historic Landmark.

INNKEEPERS:	*Rob & Joanna Jackson*
ADDRESS:	*313 Walker at Washington*
	Port Townsend, WA 98368
TELEPHONE:	*(360) 385-6753; (800) 300-6753*
FAX:	*(360) 385-2097*
E-MAIL:	*anyone@oldconsulateinn.com*
WEBSITE:	*www.oldconsulateinn.com*
ROOMS:	*5 Rooms; 3 Suites; All with private baths*
OPEN:	*Year-round*
CHILDREN:	*Children 12 and older are welcome*
ANIMALS:	*Prohibited (Exception: guide dogs)*
SMOKING:	*Prohibited*

Frittata Italiano

Makes 2 (10-inch) frittatas (8 servings each)

3/4 pound Italian sausage (weight before cooking)
1/3 cup diced (1/4-inch) onion
1/3 cup diced (1/4-inch) green bell pepper
1/3 cup diced (1/4-inch) sun-dried tomatoes
2 cloves roasted garlic, mashed (optional, but wonderful!)
2 cups cubed raw potatoes (small cubes)
10 eggs
3/4 cup sour cream
2 cups (or a little more) shredded Monterey Jack cheese
3/4 cup shredded (not grated) Parmigiano-Reggiano cheese
3 tablespoons diced pepperoncini (optional)
1 teaspoon basil
1 teaspoon oregano
Salt, to taste
Pepper, to taste
2 tablespoons butter
1/4 cup grated Parmigiano-Reggiano cheese (garnish)
1/4 cup sliced black olives (garnish)
2 sprigs fresh basil (garnish)

In a medium sauté pan, cook and lightly brown sausage. Drain. Place sausage in a small bowl to cool while preparing other ingredients. Using same pan, sauté onion and green pepper until just translucent. Add sun-dried tomatoes and garlic during last minute or two. Remove to a bowl. Sauté potatoes al dente (just until done, but not soft). Set aside. In a large bowl, beat eggs. Mix in sour cream. Add cheeses and blend. Stir in sausage, onion/pepper mixture, potatoes and pepperoncini. Season with basil, oregano, salt and pepper. PREHEAT OVEN TO 350°F. Melt butter in 2 (10-inch) ovenproof sauté pans. Divide frittata mixture between pans; cook over medium burner for approximately 10 minutes, or until edges are starting to set and center is still undone. Gently shake pans occasionally to prevent sticking. Place pans in oven for 5-10 minutes, or until center of frittata is set. Slide out onto serving platter. Cut each frittata into 8 wedges. Garnish with a sprinkling of cheese, sliced olives and fresh basil.

"We begin this breakfast with wedges of cantaloupe wrapped in prosciutto topped with crumbles of gorgonzola cheese, and offer side dishes of baked Italian link sausage, thin-sliced provolone cheese and Roma Romano tomatoes (see recipe on page 191)."

Joanna Jackson - Old Consulate Inn

Hideaway House

S tately evergreen trees greet guests as they wind their way from the ferry landing to the Hideaway House Bed and Breakfast. Located on serene Anderson Island, this secluded home offers majestic views of Mount Rainier and the natural beauty of freshwater lakes and saltwater beaches.

The romantic Angel Room has a private entrance and a jetted tub for two.

INNKEEPERS:	*Hank & Faye Lynn Hollenbaugh*
ADDRESS:	*11422 Leschi Circle*
	Anderson Island, WA 98303
TELEPHONE:	*(253) 884-4179*
FAX:	*(253) 884-2083*
E-MAIL:	*Not Available*
WEBSITE:	*Not Available*
ROOMS:	*1 Room; 1 Suite; Both with private baths*
OPEN:	*Year-round*
CHILDREN:	*Welcome*
ANIMALS:	*Welcome (Small animals)*
SMOKING:	*Permitted outside only*

Overnight Eggs

Makes 8-12 servings

1 pound link sausage, cooked and cut into bite-size pieces
6 eggs, beaten
1 cup milk
3/4 cup shredded cheddar cheese
2 plain bagels, cut into bite-size pieces
1 teaspoon dry mustard
4 green onions, thinly sliced
1/2 red pepper, chopped
Salsa (optional topping)

In a large bowl, mix together all ingredients (except salsa). Cover and refrigerate overnight.

<u>Next morning</u>: PREHEAT OVEN TO 325°F. Stir the mixture and pour into a greased 13x9-inch baking dish. Bake, uncovered, for 45 minutes. Let set for 15 minutes. Cut into squares and serve.

"I serve this with red potatoes and corn bread and offer salsa as a topping."

Faye Lynn Hollenbaugh - Hideaway House

Chambered Nautilus

T he Chambered Nautilus is a classic Seattle-style bed and breakfast
inn that combines the warmth of a country inn with excellent access
to the city's theaters, restaurants and shopping areas. Architecturally, this
Georgian Colonial reflects the English heritage of its original owners.

Catering services can be made available for events held at the inn.

INNKEEPERS:	*Joyce Schulte & Steven Poole*
ADDRESS:	*5005 22nd Avenue NE*
	Seattle, WA 98105
TELEPHONE:	*(206) 522-2536; (800) 545-8459*
FAX:	*(206) 528-0898*
E-MAIL:	*chamberednautilus@msn.com*
WEBSITE:	*www.virtualcities.com*
ROOMS:	*6 Rooms; All with private baths*
OPEN:	*Year-round*
CHILDREN:	*Children 8 and older are welcome with prior arrangement*
ANIMALS:	*Prohibited*
SMOKING:	*Prohibited*

Northwest Salmon Breakfast Pie

Makes 6 servings

Don't let the name fool you! This quiche-like treat can be served for any meal! Teamed with a fresh tossed salad or a colorful fruit plate, it will make a delightful lunch or casual dinner.

1 unbaked ready-made pie crust
1 cup chopped onion
1 clove garlic, minced
3 tablespoons butter
5 eggs, beaten
2 1/4 cups sour cream
1/4 cup flour
12 ounces cooked salmon, skin and bones removed, flaked
1 1/2 cups shredded Swiss cheese, divided
1 teaspoon dried dill weed
Paprika (optional)

PREHEAT OVEN TO 400°F. Bake pie crust in a regular 10-inch pie plate (or a deep-dish 9-inch pie plate) for 8 minutes; remove from oven. Lower oven temperature to 375°F. In a small pan, sauté onion and garlic in butter until tender. In a large bowl, combine beaten eggs, sour cream and flour. Stir in onion mixture and flaked salmon. Stir in 1 cup of cheese and dill weed. Pour filling into partially-baked crust. Sprinkle with remaining 1/2 cup cheese. Sprinkle with a little paprika for color, if desired. Bake at 375°F. for 45-50 minutes (if using the deep-dish pie plate, bake for 55-60 minutes). Cover with foil the last 15 minutes of baking time. Bake until knife inserted in center comes out clean. Let stand 15 minutes before serving.

Glenna's Guthrie Cottage

G lenna's Guthrie Cottage is a rare bed and breakfast inn that offers
cooking classes for its guests. Innkeeper Glenna O'Neil is a
member of the American Culinary Federation, and her classes range from
"Cooking by the Seat of Your Pants" for beginning cooks to low fat/low
cholesterol meals, stir fry, vegetarian and Italian.

A gift area showcases antiques, quilts, dolls, tapestries, thimbles, teapots,
coffees, etc.

INNKEEPERS:	*Jack & Glenna O'Neil*
ADDRESS:	*10083 Old Olympic Highway*
	Sequim, WA 98382
TELEPHONE:	*(360) 681-4349; (800) 930-4349*
FAX:	*(360) 681-4349*
E-MAIL:	*glennas.olypen.com*
WEBSITE:	*www.olypen.com/glennas*
ROOMS:	*4 Rooms; 2 Suites; Private and shared baths*
OPEN:	*Year-round*
CHILDREN:	*Welcome*
ANIMALS:	*Prohibited*
SMOKING:	*Permitted outside in designated areas*

Impossible Crab Pie

Makes 6 servings

1/2 pound fresh <u>or</u> 1 (6-ounce) can crabmeat, drained
1/2 cup grated cheddar cheese
**1 (3-ounce) package cream cheese, room
    temperature**
1/4 cup diced green onion
1 (2-ounce) jar diced pimientos
1 cup milk
1/2 cup baking mix (such as Bisquick)
2 eggs
Salt, to taste
Dash of nutmeg

PREHEAT OVEN TO 350°F. In a large bowl, mix together crab, grated cheese, cream cheese, green onion and pimientos. In a blender, combine milk, baking mix, eggs, salt and nutmeg. Blend on high speed for 15 seconds, then mix with crab mixture. Spoon mixture into a greased casserole dish. Place casserole dish in a pan with hot water and bake for 40 minutes.

Outlook

The Outlook Bed and Breakfast is a 1910 vintage Craftsman home with a 180 degree unobstructed view of Mount Baker, Guemes Channel and the San Juan Islands. The beautifully landscaped yard features camellias, azaleas and 28 rhododendrons.

From the deck or cozy living area, guests often observe bald eagles, seals, sea lions, otters and an occasional whale or orca.

INNKEEPERS:	*Trish Robinson*
ADDRESS:	*608 H Avenue*
	Anacortes, WA 98221
TELEPHONE:	*(360) 293-3505; (888) 634-5844*
FAX:	*Not Available*
E-MAIL:	*Not Available*
WEBSITE:	*www.whidbey.com/outlook/*
ROOMS:	*2 Rooms; Private baths*
OPEN:	*Year-round*
CHILDREN:	*Children over the age of 12 are welcome*
ANIMALS:	*Prohibited*
SMOKING:	*Permitted on outdoor deck or porch*

Broccoli-Bacon Quiche

Makes 4-6 servings

4 eggs
1 cup half-and-half
1 cup grated Swiss cheese
2 cups broccoli florets, partially cooked 2-3 minutes
4 slices bacon, cooked and crumbled, divided
1/4 teaspoon salt
1/8 teaspoon garlic powder
1/8 teaspoon lemon pepper (or black pepper)

PREHEAT OVEN TO 350°F. In a large bowl, beat together eggs and half-and-half. Stir in cheese, broccoli, half of the bacon, salt, garlic powder and lemon pepper. Coat a 9-inch pie plate with nonstick cooking spray. Pour egg mixture into pie plate and bake uncovered for 30-35 minutes, or until done. Let set a few minutes before cutting into serving pieces. Top with remaining crumbled bacon for garnish.

"I cook the bacon in the microwave the evening before I serve it for breakfast. I also parboil the broccoli in the microwave for two minutes, drain, and refrigerate it overnight. It makes it very quick to assemble in the morning. The quiche can be served cold, but I think it is much better when served hot."

Trish Robinson - Outlook Bed & Breakfast

Caswell's on the Bay

C aswell's on the Bay Bed and Breakfast is a grand, two-story turreted Victorian encircled by a covered verandah that showcases colorful flower pots and hanging baskets. The rooms are spacious, providing a wondrous setting to display quality antiques, floral and country garden watercolors and Tiffany-style stained glass lamps.

The beautifully presented breakfasts sometimes include oysters from the Willapa Bay area.

INNKEEPERS:	*Bob & Marilyn Caswell*
ADDRESS:	*25204 Sandridge Road*
	Ocean Park, WA 98640
TELEPHONE:	*(360) 665-6535*
FAX:	*(360) 665-6500*
E-MAIL:	*Not Available*
WEBSITE:	*www.site-works.com/caswells*
ROOMS:	*5 Rooms; All with private baths*
OPEN:	*Year-round*
CHILDREN:	*Children over the age of 12 are welcome*
ANIMALS:	*Prohibited*
SMOKING:	*Permitted outside only*

Shredded Potato Quiche

Makes 8 servings

"Real men" <u>do</u> eat quiche and here's a very hearty and flavorful one! Start this recipe the night before you plan to serve it.

3 to 4 cups (12 to 16-ounces) frozen seasoned shredded potatoes (<u>tiny</u> Tater Tots or
    Crispy Crowns work great!)
1/4 cup grated Parmesan cheese
1/2 cup sliced green onions
1/2 cup shredded Swiss cheese
1/2 cup shredded Monterey Jack cheese
1 cup shredded cheddar cheese
1/2 pound bacon (8-10 slices), cooked and crumbled
1 (3-ounce) can sliced mushrooms, drained
1/4 cup (or more) sliced zucchini
1/4 cup (or more) diced yellow or red bell pepper
5 eggs
2 cups half-and-half
3/4 teaspoon salt
1/4 teaspoon sugar
1/8 teaspoon cayenne pepper

PREHEAT BROILER. Coat a 10-inch pie plate with nonstick cooking spray. Place potatoes in pie plate and broil, stirring occasionally, until all sides of potatoes are browned. Mash potatoes with fork to cover bottom of dish. Over potatoes, layer Parmesan cheese, green onions, Swiss cheese, Monterey Jack cheese, cheddar cheese, bacon, mushrooms, zucchini and bell pepper. Cover and refrigerate overnight.

<u>Next morning</u>: PREHEAT OVEN TO 375°F. In a large bowl, beat together eggs, half-and-half, salt, sugar and cayenne pepper. Pour egg mixture slowly over top of refrigerated quiche ingredients. Bake 50-60 minutes, or until golden brown and knife inserted in center comes out clean. Remove from oven and let stand for 20 minutes before serving.

Carol's Corner

To keep from spilling, place the pie plate in the oven before completely filling with the egg mixture. Pour in the last cupful while dish is on the oven rack. Don't be alarmed if all of the egg mixture doesn't quite fit (it all depends on your actual dish size and the amount of potatoes and vegetables you use). It will still turn out great! Marilyn, at Caswell's on the Bay, suggests leaving out the bacon for vegetarian guests. She also says chopped artichokes (not marinated) are a delicious addition to this quiche.

Fruit Specialties

Fruit
Specialties

Bosch Gärten

B uilt in 1992 specifically as a bed and breakfast facility, Bosch Gärten provides a quiet getaway with the magnificent Cascade Mountains towering in the background. Guests enjoy the living room with its 30-foot ceiling, distinctive fireplace and 18-foot potted Norfolk pine.

The fresh, multi-course breakfast features Leavenworth's fabulous tree fruits and pastries, juice, tea and freshly ground Starbucks coffee.

INNKEEPERS:	*Cal & Myke Bosch*
ADDRESS:	*9846 Dye Road*
	Leavenworth, WA 98826
TELEPHONE:	*(509) 548-6900; (800) 535-0069*
FAX:	*(509) 548-6076*
EMAIL:	*Not Available*
WEBSITE:	*www.boschgärten.com*
ROOMS:	*3 Rooms; All with private baths*
OPEN:	*Year-round*
CHILDREN:	*School age children are welcome*
ANIMALS:	*Prohibited*
SMOKING:	*Prohibited*

Fresh Fruit with Amaretto Cream

Makes 4 servings

1 1/2 tablespoons amaretto liqueur
2 tablespoons dark brown sugar
1/2 cup sour cream
2 cups cut-up fresh fruit

In a small bowl, stir together liqueur and brown sugar. Add sour cream and mix thoroughly. Let stand in refrigerator 2 hours before serving. Place 1/2 cup fruit into each serving dish (use pretty sherbet glasses). Drizzle with sauce just before serving.

"I use blueberries, green grapes, apples, pears, peaches,
bananas and strawberries - any combination of fresh fruit.
The sauce keeps for two weeks, so I make double batches."

Myke Bosch - Bosch Gärten Bed & Breakfast

Salisbury House

L ocated only minutes from downtown Seattle, the University of Washington and Seattle University, the Salisbury House Bed and Breakfast Inn offers gracious "in-city" accommodations for the discerning traveler. Shops, restaurants and parks are all within walking distance.

This exquisite urban bed and breakfast inn is operated by a mother-daughter team.

INNKEEPERS:	*Cathryn & Mary Wiese*
ADDRESS:	*750 16th Avenue East*
	Seattle, WA 98112
TELEPHONE:	*(206) 328-8682*
FAX:	*(206) 720-1019*
EMAIL:	*cathy@salisburyhouse.com*
WEBSITE:	*www.salisburyhouse.com*
ROOMS:	*4 Rooms; All with private baths*
OPEN:	*Year-round*
CHILDREN:	*Children over the age of 12 are welcome*
ANIMALS:	*Prohibited*
SMOKING:	*Prohibited*

Chunky Applesauce

Makes 4 servings

3 Golden Delicious apples, peeled, cored and sliced
1/3 cup water
1/4 cup sugar (or more to taste)
1/2 teaspoon ground cinnamon (or more to taste)

In a medium saucepan, combine apples with water. Cook over low heat until apples are soft but still hold together, about 12-15 minutes. Stir in sugar and cinnamon. Applesauce may be served hot or cold.

Hanford Castle

L ooming mirage-like from its lofty hilltop location, the Hanford Castle Bed and Breakfast is a historic, turn-of-the-century castle surrounded by a sea of Palouse wheatlands. Devoted to authenticity, the owners showcase a Victorian pump organ in the parlor, antique kerosene lighting and an indoor garden and fountain, complete with a "witches ball."

The castle is undergoing a complete restoration.

INNKEEPERS:	*Paul Matthews & Terri Gravelle*
ADDRESS:	*PO Box 23*
	Oakesdale, WA 99158
TELEPHONE:	*(509) 285-4120*
FAX:	*Not Available*
EMAIL:	*Not Available*
WEBSITE:	*Not Available*
ROOMS:	*2 Rooms; Private baths*
OPEN:	*Year-round*
CHILDREN:	*Prohibited*
ANIMALS:	*Prohibited*
SMOKING:	*Permitted outside only*

Peaches Supreme

Makes 3-6 servings

1/2 cup brown sugar + 6 teaspoons brown sugar, divided
1/2 cup chopped pecans
1/2 cup butter, melted
1/2 cup rolled oats
1/2 cup granola (with dates and raisins)
1 (20-ounce) can peach halves, drained (usually
   6 halves)
1 (6-ounce) container custard-style vanilla yogurt
8 tablespoons raspberry jam (homemade freezer
   jam is best)

PREHEAT BROILER. To prepare topping: In a small bowl, combine 1/2 cup brown sugar, pecans, butter, oats and granola. Mix well and set aside. Arrange peach halves, rounded-sides down, in shallow baking dish (a pie plate works fine). Place one teaspoon of brown sugar in each peach. Broil for 2-3 minutes. Watch carefully! Remove from broiler and place a large, heaping spoonful of topping on each peach. Broil an additional 1-3 minutes, or until topping begins to turn brown - again, watch carefully! Remove from broiler and top each peach half with a tablespoon of vanilla yogurt and a tablespoon of jam.

Serving suggestion: Attractively arrange each peach half on a bed of green leafy lettuce. Very colorful!

A Touch of Europe

O riginally built in 1889 by one of Yakima's prominent pioneers,
A Touch of Europe Bed and Breakfast Inn eventually became the
home of Mrs. Ina Phillips Williams, Yakima County's first woman
legislator in the Washington State House of Representatives. Every room
is rich in history. Theodore Roosevelt once met with Mrs. Williams
in the library.

This Queen Anne Victorian house is on the National Register of
Historic Places.

INNKEEPERS: *Erika G. & James A. Cenci*
ADDRESS: *220 North 16th Avenue*
Yakima, WA 98902
TELEPHONE: *(509) 454-9775; (888) 438-7073*
FAX: *Not Available*
EMAIL: *Not Available*
WEBSITE: *www.winesnw.com/toucheuropeb&b.htm*
ROOMS: *3 Rooms; All with private baths*
OPEN: *Year-round*
CHILDREN: *Prohibited*
ANIMALS: *Prohibited*
SMOKING: *Permitted outside only*

Signature Pears in Amaretto with Chocolate Sauce

Makes 4 servings

4 large pears
Cold water
Juice of 1 lemon
4 tablespoons sugar
1 cup water
4 tablespoons amaretto liqueur
1 cup chocolate sauce, warm (recipe to follow)
Whipped cream, for garnish
Peppermint leaves, for garnish
1/2 cup sliced almonds, for garnish

Carefully peel pears, leaving stems intact. Place peeled whole pears in a large bowl. Fill with cold water and add lemon juice. Set aside. In a large saucepan, bring sugar and water to a boil over moderate heat. Drain pears and place them on their sides in the sugar water. Add liqueur and simmer, covered, for 20 minutes. Carefully transfer pears to a serving dish and ladle sugar water/liqueur mixture over them. Let pears cool, then cover and refrigerate overnight. Drain pears before serving.

For a beautiful presentation: Place each pear in an individual glass dish, then set each dish on top of a big plate. Serve with warm chocolate sauce, a dollop of whipped cream and garnish with mint leaves and almond slices.

Chocolate Sauce
8 ounces semi-sweet chocolate, cut into bits
1/2 cup strong brewed coffee
1 teaspoon amaretto liqueur or cognac

In top of double boiler over hot water, melt chocolate with coffee and liqueur. Keep sauce warm over hot water until serving time. If sauce becomes too thick, add more coffee. Note: Recipe may be doubled.

> ### Carol's Corner
>
> *Be sure everyone has a knife, fork and small spoon when you serve this special treat so that every last bite of pear and spoonful of sauce can be savored!*

 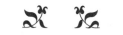  

Lietz's

L ietz's Bed and Breakfast is a cozy country inn located four and one-half miles east of Leavenworth on the Wenatchee River. Guests savor the delicious, family-style breakfast that is served each morning from seven to ten o'clock.

Due to the close proximity of the Wenatchee River, guests can experience venturesome innertube float trips, the innertubes being provided by the inn.

INNKEEPERS:	*Verne & Helen Lietz*
ADDRESS:	*8305 Lynn Street*
	Peshastin, WA 98847
TELEPHONE:	*(509) 548-7504*
FAX:	*Not Available*
EMAIL:	*Not Available*
WEBSITE:	*Not Available*
ROOMS:	*3 Rooms; Shared baths*
OPEN:	*Year-round*
CHILDREN:	*Welcome*
ANIMALS:	*Prohibited*
SMOKING:	*Prohibited*

Pears Extraordinaire

Makes 2 servings

The rich, red color of the berries in contrast to the green of the mint leaves makes for a beautiful presentation.

1 fresh pear, cut in half, peeled and cored
2 tablespoons apple juice or your favorite liqueur (green-colored crème de menthe is great at Christmas)
1 tablespoon cream cheese, room temperature
1 teaspoon honey
1/4 teaspoon vanilla
Fresh red raspberries or strawberries, for garnish
Fresh mint leaves, for garnish

In a small microwave-safe dish, place pear halves cut-side down. Add apple juice or liqueur. Cover with plastic wrap and microwave for 4-5 minutes to poach the pear until soft, but not mushy. Drain off any liquid. Place each half, cut-side up, on individual serving plates. <u>To prepare filling</u>: In a small bowl, mix together cream cheese, honey and vanilla. Spoon half of mixture into center of each pear half. Garnish with fresh berries and mint leaves.

Stratford Manor

G uests of the Stratford Manor Bed and Breakfast can schedule a relaxing and soothing massage. The licensed massage therapist is experienced in Swedish Deep Tissue and Sport Massage and customizes his sessions to specific pains or just for mental and physical relaxation.

Sessions are for one hour or a couple's special that includes two, 45-minute massages.

INNKEEPERS:	*Leslie & Jim Lohse*
ADDRESS:	*1416 VanWyck Road*
	Bellingham, WA 98226
TELEPHONE:	*(360) 715-8441*
FAX:	*(360) 671-0840*
WEBSITE:	*llohse@aol.com*
EMAIL:	*www.site-works.com/stratford*
ROOMS:	*3 Rooms; All with private baths*
OPEN:	*Year-round*
CHILDREN:	*Prohibited*
ANIMALS:	*Prohibited*
SMOKING:	*Permitted on outside porch only*

Winter Fruit Compote

Makes 4 servings

8 dried pitted prunes
8 dried apricots
1 cup apple juice
1 cinnamon stick
1/2 teaspoon whole cloves
1/2 cup orange juice
3 tablespoons orange marmalade
1 banana, peeled and sliced
1 orange, peeled and cut-up
1 apple, peeled and diced
Chopped pecans, for garnish

In a medium saucepan, combine prunes, apricots, apple juice, cinnamon stick and cloves. Bring to a boil and remove from heat. Refrigerate; let the prunes and apricots soak in the apple juice mixture overnight.

Next morning: Place 2 prunes and 2 apricots in each of 4 serving dishes. Strain the apple juice mixture. Add orange juice and orange marmalade to strained mixture. Add cut-up fresh fruit. Divide between the 4 dishes. Top each serving with chopped pecans.

Redfern Farm

R edfern Farm Bed and Breakfast is a 50-year-old steeply gabled farmhouse surrounded by 20 acres of pasture on Puget Island in the Columbia River. The island was named in 1792 after Peter Puget and is one of a handful of the hundreds of islands in the Columbia River estuary. Drainage sloughs and a perimeter dike protect the island.

Access to the island is either by bridge from Cathlamet, Washington or by ferry from Westport, Oregon.

INNKEEPERS:	*Winnie Lowsma*
ADDRESS:	*277 Cross Dike Road*
	Cathlamet, WA 98612
TELEPHONE:	*(360) 849-4108*
FAX:	*Not Available*
EMAIL:	*Not Available*
WEBSITE:	*Not Available*
ROOMS:	*2 Rooms; Private baths*
OPEN:	*Year-round*
CHILDREN:	*Children six and older are welcome*
ANIMALS:	*Prohibited*
SMOKING:	*Prohibited*

Apple Meringue Cassolette

Makes 2 servings

A light sweetness to start the day!

1 tablespoon frozen apple juice concentrate
3 tablespoons water
1 teaspoon cornstarch
1 medium apple, peeled, cored and diced
2 egg whites, room temperature
1 to 2 teaspoons sugar
Dash of cinnamon
Sprinkle of coconut

PREHEAT OVEN TO 350°F. In a small saucepan, combine apple juice concentrate, water and cornstarch. Mix well using a mini whisk. Cook over medium heat until mixture is clear, bubbling and thickened, stirring constantly. Add apples and mix to coat with sauce. Set aside. To make meringue: In a small bowl, beat egg whites. Add sugar and beat until stiff (whites should hold their shape). Set aside. Divide the apple mixture between two small, ungreased cassolette dishes (or ramekins or custard cups). Dust lightly with cinnamon. Using a small spatula, spread half the meringue over top of each filled dish, sealing the egg white mixture to rim of dish. Sprinkle a little coconut over the meringue. Place dishes on a baking sheet and bake for 8-10 minutes, or until tops are nicely browned.

Carol's Corner

For a very special first course at breakfast, place each ramekin on top of a colorful plate, complete with paper doily. Or if you prefer, serve the Apple Meringue Cassolette on a larger plate accompanied by perhaps an egg dish and muffin. Served later in the day with a cookie, this would make a delightful, light dessert. So versatile!

Hideaway House

The Hideaway House Bed and Breakfast offers old-fashioned hospitality in a quiet country setting. Located in the heart of Anderson Island, this secluded home offers majestic views of Mount Rainier and the natural beauty of freshwater lakes and saltwater beaches.

A full country breakfast is served in the family dining area or on the cedar deck that overlooks the surrounding woods.

INNKEEPERS: *Hank & Faye Lynn Hollenbaugh*
ADDRESS: *11422 Leschi Circle*
Anderson Island, WA 98303
TELEPHONE: *(253) 884-4179*
FAX: *(253) 884-2083*
EMAIL: *Not Available*
WEBSITE: *Not Available*
ROOMS: *1 Room; 1 Suite; Private baths*
OPEN: *Year-round*
CHILDREN: *Children of all ages are welcome*
ANIMALS: *Small animals are welcome*
SMOKING: *Permitted outside only*

Hawaiian Cream Fruit Salad

Makes 8-10 servings

1 (20-ounce) can pineapple tidbits
1 (11-ounce) can mandarin orange segments
1 (16-ounce) can peach slices
1 (16-ounce) can pear slices
1 apple
1 banana
1 (3.4-ounce) package vanilla instant pudding mix
1 1/2 cups milk
1/3 of (6-ounce) can frozen orange juice concentrate
3/4 cup sour cream

Drain all canned fruit well. Cut canned fruit and fresh fruit into bite-size pieces and place in a large bowl. Set aside. In a small bowl, beat together pudding mix, milk and orange juice concentrate for 2 minutes. Add sour cream and mix thoroughly. Pour pudding mixture over fruit and stir to coat. Cover and refrigerate at least 2 hours.

The Purple House

G uests take a trip back-in-time to a gentler, more gracious way of living when they stay at The Purple House Bed and Breakfast. This elegantly remodeled Queen Anne mansion was built in 1882 by Dr. Pietrzycki, a Dayton pioneer physician and philanthropist.

The city of Dayton is a historic gem, boasting two complete districts on the National Historic Register and dozens of well-preserved Victorian homes.

INNKEEPERS:	*D. Christine Williscroft*
ADDRESS:	*415 East Clay Street*
	Dayton, WA 99328
TELEPHONE:	*(509) 382-3159; (800) 486-2574*
FAX:	*Not Available*
EMAIL:	*Not Available*
WEBSITE:	*Not Available*
ROOMS:	*4 Rooms; 2 Suites; Private and shared baths*
OPEN:	*Year-round*
CHILDREN:	*Welcome*
ANIMALS:	*Welcome*
SMOKING:	*Prohibited*

Pretty and Tasty Fruit Tart

Makes 6 servings

This pastry, sprinkled with powdered sugar, may be served warm for breakfast, or try it chilled, topped with whipped cream, for an afternoon dessert with coffee or tea.

1/2 cup (1 stick) butter, room temperature
2 tablespoons sugar
1 cup flour
1 egg yolk
3 to 4 fresh apricots, halved and pitted (plums or thinly sliced apples can also be used)

Filling

2 eggs
2 tablespoons milk
2 tablespoons sugar
5 drops (about 1/16 teaspoon) almond extract
Whipped cream or powdered sugar, for garnish

PREHEAT OVEN TO 375°F. To make dough: In a medium bowl, mix together butter, sugar, flour and egg yolk. Set aside. To make filling: In a small bowl, beat together eggs, milk, sugar and almond extract. Set aside. Press dough into a lightly greased 9x4-inch fluted tart pan. Arrange apricot halves (skin-side down, dimple-side up) or other fruit over dough. Pour filling mixture over fruit and dough (fill the dimples). Bake for approximately 45 minutes. Let cool for at least 15 minutes before serving. May be served warm or cold.

Side Dishes

Side Dishes

Chinaberry Hill

F ormerly the Lucius Manning Estate, Chinaberry Hill was best known at the turn-of-the-century for its breathtaking gardens. Filled with antiques and Tacoma memorabilia, this graceful Victorian is on the National Register of Historic Places.

"Put Chinaberry Hill on wheels, and we'd take it on all our vacations."

~ Guest, Chinaberry Hill

INNKEEPERS:	*Cecil & Yarrow Wayman*
ADDRESS:	*302 Tacoma Avenue North*
	North Tacoma, WA 98403
TELEPHONE:	*(253) 272-1282*
FAX:	*(253) 272-1335*
EMAIL:	*chinaberry@wa.net*
WEBSITE:	*www.wa.net/chinaberry*
ROOMS:	*1 Room; 4 Suites; All with private baths*
OPEN:	*Year-round*
CHILDREN:	*Children are welcome in the guest cottage*
ANIMALS:	*Prohibited; Resident cats*
SMOKING:	*Permitted on verandah*

Garlic Potatoes

Makes 4-6 servings

8 small to medium potatoes (red or Yukon gold potatoes are great)
3 tablespoons butter
2 teaspoons Lawry's garlic salt
1 teaspoon coarse ground pepper
3 tablespoons fresh chopped parsley

Cut potatoes into small bite-sized cubes. Rinse well and pat dry. Put butter into a 12-inch skillet over medium-high to high heat; add the potatoes before butter is completely melted. Cover and cook about 2 to 3 minutes. Pull lid and check to see if potatoes are browning. They should be getting pretty crispy. Check every minute or so, and stir them from the bottom every time. When potatoes are nicely browned, turn burner down to low for holding. Just before serving, add garlic salt, pepper and parsley. Note: The critical point is to add the garlic salt <u>just before serving</u> for maximum impact.

"This recipe, rather embarrassingly simple, never fails to wow the crowd. Once again, as Julia Child loves to point out, people crave "foody food", and that the simplest approach is often the best."

Cecil Wayman - Chinaberry Hill

Inn at Barnum Point

In her childhood, innkeeper Carolin Barnum Dilorenzo played on the Camano Island beach and swam and boated in Port Susan Bay. As an adult, she built a beautiful home on the edge of an orchard that overlooks Port Susan Bay and now offers her home as The Inn at Barnum Point.

On clear days, the inn offers spectacular views of Mount Rainier and the Cascades.

INNKEEPERS:	*Carolin Barnum Dilorenzo*
ADDRESS:	*464 South Barnum Road*
	Camano Island, WA 98292
TELEPHONE:	*(360) 387-2256; (800) 910-2256*
FAX:	*(360) 387-2256*
EMAIL:	*Not Available*
WEBSITE:	*www.whidbey.com/inn/*
ROOMS:	*2 Rooms; Private baths*
OPEN:	*Year-round*
CHILDREN:	*Welcome*
ANIMALS:	*Prohibited*
SMOKING:	*Prohibited*

Barnum Point Potato Special

Makes 2 servings

2 cups cooked and diced red potatoes (with skins)
1 tablespoon vegetable or olive oil
1 small onion, diced
1/2 cup (total) diced green, red, orange and yellow peppers
1/2 cup diced ham
Salt and pepper (optional)
1/2 cup grated Monterey Jack cheese
1/2 cup grated cheddar cheese
Sour cream
Salsa

PREHEAT OVEN TO 350°F. In a medium ovenproof skillet, fry potatoes in oil until browned. Add onion and peppers and cook until soft. Add ham and heat through. Season with salt and pepper, if desired. Top with cheeses and place in oven until cheese is melted. Transfer to individual serving plates or serve directly from hot skillet at table. (Note: If you prefer, the potatoes could also be divided between two individual ovenproof serving dishes before putting in oven.) Serve with sour cream and salsa on the side.

Four Winds Guest House

Located within walking distance of the mighty Grand Coulee Dam, the Four Winds Guest House Bed and Breakfast evokes another era in its 1930's charm and spectacular setting. Originally a dormitory for male engineers working on the Grand Coulee Dam, this historic building is the last of the government built homes open to the public.

Grand Coulee Dam is home to the world's largest laser light show.

INNKEEPERS:	*Dick & Fe Taylor*
ADDRESS:	*301 Lincoln Street*
	Coulee Dam, WA 99116
TELEPHONE:	*(509) 633-3146; (800) 786-3146*
FAX:	*(509) 633-2454*
EMAIL:	*fourwind@televar.com*
WEBSITE:	*Not Available*
ROOMS:	*11 Rooms; 1 Suite; Private and shared baths*
OPEN:	*Year-round*
CHILDREN:	*Welcome (Call ahead for guidelines)*
ANIMALS:	*Prohibited*
SMOKING:	*Permitted outside only*

Comeback Hash

Makes 6 servings

A very colorful, hearty dish!

4 tablespoons (1/2 stick) margarine
1 (2-pound) bag frozen southern-style hash brown potatoes
Oregano, to taste
Thyme, to taste
Basil, to taste
Garlic powder, to taste
1 medium onion, diced
1/2 green bell pepper, diced
1/2 red bell pepper, diced
5 precooked German sausages (about 4-ounces each), diced
1 (16-ounce) bag frozen corn kernels
Salsa (optional)

In a large skillet over medium-high heat, melt margarine and add potatoes, spreading evenly. Add spices on top. Do not disturb until crisp enough to turn; then finish to crispness desired. (Try not to cook to "mush".) In another large skillet, sauté onion and peppers. Add diced sausage and corn and cook until thoroughly heated. Add sausage/vegetable mixture to potatoes and stir gently to mix all ingredients. Cover and reduce heat to "warm" and marry flavors for 20-30 minutes before serving. Serve plain or with salsa.

Cedar House Inn

The Cedar House Inn Bed and Breakfast is located on Point Roberts, a 3.9 square mile peninsula. This beautiful home has cathedral ceilings and a floor-to-ceiling brick fireplace. Magnificent evergreen trees surround the rear deck.

Guests enjoy exploring the surrounding wooded areas where they can pick ferns, flowers, blackberries or tiptoe through the coast's largest heron rookery.

INNKEEPERS:	*Amos & Nancy Heacock*
ADDRESS:	*1534 Gulf Road*
	Point Roberts, WA 98281
TELEPHONE:	*(360) 945-0284*
FAX:	*Not Available*
EMAIL:	*Not Available*
WEBSITE:	*Not Available*
ROOMS:	*6 Rooms; Private and shared baths*
OPEN:	*Year-round*
CHILDREN:	*Welcome*
ANIMALS:	*Welcome*
SMOKING:	*Permitted on outside deck only*

Happy Sausage Wheels

Makes 8 servings

A very unique and tasty side dish! Add scrambled eggs, a muffin or scone and a colorful fruit cup for a very special breakfast.

2 pounds bulk pork sausage
2 small onions, chopped
2 cups peeled and diced apples
2 cups bread crumbs
Salt, to taste
Pepper, to taste
Sage, to taste

PREHEAT OVEN TO 350°F. Place sausage on piece of aluminum foil and roll out or hand pat until it spreads into a 1/2-inch-thick rectangle, approximately 10x12-inches. In a large bowl, mix together onions, apples, bread crumbs, salt, pepper and sage. Distribute mixture evenly over sausage. Starting with 12-inch side, roll sausage jelly-roll fashion, pinching sausage at seam to seal. Use foil to help form the roll, pulling it back from sausage as roll takes shape. Place sausage roll into baking pan (using two spatulas may be helpful). Bake for 60 minutes. Remove from oven and let rest 5 minutes. Place sausage roll on cutting board (use spatulas again). Using a sharp, serrated knife, cut serving slices (about 8) and place onto individual serving plates. As you lay them on their sides, the "wheel" will show.

"Everybody loves our breakfasts which sometimes last one to two hours, just sitting at the table visiting like family. We serve big breakfasts and find out ahead of time what our guests like. We run a family bed and breakfast and each day add to our enormous roster of good friends. It's such a lovely, satisfying work to be in!"

Nancy Heacock - Cedar House Inn

Heaven's Edge

T he Heaven's Edge Bed and Breakfast is a private waterfront estate that overlooks the Olympic Mountains where the Hood Canal meets Dahob Bay. This romantic waterfront escape offers privacy, security, relaxation and natural beauty.

Guest amenities include fresh flowers, fruit, feather pillows and down comforters.

INNKEEPERS:	*Mary Lee Duley*
ADDRESS:	*7410 NW Ioka Drive*
	Silverdale, WA 98383
TELEPHONE:	*(360) 613-1111; (800) 413-5680*
FAX:	*(360) 692-4444*
EMAIL:	*heaven@tscnet.com*
WEBSITE:	*www.kitsap.net/business/bnb/heaven*
ROOMS:	*2 Suites; Private baths*
OPEN:	*Year-round*
CHILDREN:	*Children 16 and over are welcome*
ANIMALS:	*Prohibited*
SMOKING:	*Prohibited*

Corn Fritters

Makes 8 large or 16 small fritters

1 3/4 cups flour
2 teaspoons baking powder
3/4 teaspoon salt
1 egg, beaten
3/4 cup milk
1 cup whole kernel corn, drained
1 tablespoon butter, melted
Melted shortening, for frying
Maple syrup (optional)

In a large bowl, sift together flour, baking powder and salt. Set aside. In a small bowl, combine egg, milk, corn and butter. Add wet ingredients to dry ingredients and stir until just combined. Melt shortening (to one-inch depth) in skillet. Drop spoonfuls of batter into hot shortening and fry for 4-5 minutes, turning once, until fritters are golden brown and cooked through. Drain on paper towels. If desired, serve with warm maple syrup.

Old Consulate Inn
(F.W. Hastings House)

S itting high on a bluff with commanding views of Mount Rainier and the Olympic Mountains, the Old Consulate Inn is Port Townsend's founding family mansion. Originally built in 1889 by Senator F.W. Hastings, this grand mansion has become one of the most photographed and artistically depicted Victorians in the Pacific Northwest.

The Old Consulate Inn is a designated National Historic Landmark.

INNKEEPERS:	*Rob & Joanna Jackson*
ADDRESS:	*313 Walker at Washington*
	Port Townsend, WA 98368
TELEPHONE:	*(360) 385-6753; (800) 300-6753*
FAX:	*(360) 385-2097*
EMAIL:	*anyone@oldconsulateinn.com*
WEBSITE:	*www.oldconsulateinn.com*
ROOMS:	*5 Rooms; 3 Suites; All with private baths*
OPEN:	*Year-round*
CHILDREN:	*Children 12 and older are welcome*
ANIMALS:	*Prohibited (Exception: guide dogs)*
SMOKING:	*Prohibited*

Roma Romano Tomatoes

Makes 8 servings as a side dish (24 tomato halves)

12 small to medium Roma tomatoes
6 tablespoons butter, melted
6 tablespoons grated Romano cheese
2 tablespoons dried basil

PREHEAT BROILER. Using a fluting or small paring knife, cut each tomato in half from stem to bud (lengthwise) by making small "V" shaped cuts towards center of fruit. Place tomato halves on rimmed cookie sheet or shallow baking dish. Drizzle butter into each half. Sprinkle with grated cheese and a pinch of basil. Place in oven on second shelf under broiler. Broil approximately 5 minutes, or until bubbly and browned. Serve hot.

> **Carol's Corner**
>
> *By making V-shaped cuts to the middle of the tomato all the way around when cutting the tomato in half, a pretty zigzag edge is formed. The resulting ridges also help keep the melted butter from running off the tomato.*

Domaine Madeleine

T he Ming Room at the Domaine Madeleine Bed and Breakfast
occupies the entire top floor of the main house. The 30-foot balcony
affords spectacular views of the Strait of Juan De Fuca and the lights
of Victoria.

"A blend of Asian artistry with pampering à la Francaise; breakfast is a
visual and culinary triumph. Truly a museum-caliber B & B."

~ Guest, Domaine Madeleine

INNKEEPERS: *Madeleine & John Chambers*
ADDRESS: *146 Wildflower Lane*
Port Angeles, WA 98362
TELEPHONE: *(360) 457-4174*
FAX: *(360) 457-3037*
EMAIL: *domm@olypen.com*
WEBSITE: *www.northolympic.com/dm*
ROOMS: *1 Room; 3 Suites; 1 Cottage; All with private baths*
OPEN: *Year-round*
CHILDREN: *Children over the age of 12 are welcome*
ANIMALS: *Prohibited*
SMOKING: *Permitted outdoors only*

Ratatouille

Makes 6 servings

A luscious medley of flavors and colors! For convenience, you may use the sweet roasted peppers that come in a jar.

1 pound eggplant, thinly sliced or diced
Salt
Flour
1/2 cup olive oil, divided
1 pound zucchini, sliced
1 pound onions, peeled and thinly sliced
3 red bell peppers, roasted, peeled, seeded, cut into strips
5 garlic cloves, peeled and crushed
1 1/2 pounds tomatoes, skinned, seeded, coarsely chopped
Salt and freshly ground black pepper, to taste
2 fresh thyme sprigs (or 1 teaspoon dried)
5 large fresh basil leaves, chopped (or 1 tablespoon dried)
Chopped fresh parsley, for garnish

Sprinkle eggplant with salt and drain after 20 minutes (salt will draw moisture out). Pat dry and sprinkle lightly with flour. Heat half the oil (1/4 cup) in a large heavy pan. Add eggplant and fry over moderate heat until lightly colored, stirring frequently. Add zucchini and continue frying for 5-6 minutes until lightly colored. Remove both eggplant and zucchini with slotted spoon and set aside. Add remaining oil to pan, then add onions and fry gently until soft. Add peppers and garlic, increase heat and fry for a few minutes. Add tomatoes and cook gently for 10 minutes, stirring frequently. Return eggplant and zucchini to pan; stir well to mix with other vegetables. Add salt and pepper to taste; crumble in thyme. Cook gently, uncovered, for 20 minutes or until vegetables are soft, stirring occasionally. Just before serving, add basil to ratatouille, taste and adjust seasoning. Transfer to a warmed serving dish and sprinkle with parsley. Serve hot or cold.

Carol's Corner

This is a versatile dish! To use as a main dish, add slices of Italian sausage. Ratatouille served at room temperature with crackers makes a nice appetizer. (Make it a day in advance - it gets even better, as the flavors have a chance to blend.) To use ratatouille as an omelet filling, see Madeleine's creative recipe on page 143.

St. Helens Manorhouse

Originally built in 1910, the St. Helens Manorhouse Bed and Breakfast boasts original wavy, etched, stained and beveled glasswork. This countryside haven features beautiful woodwork and elegantly appointed guest rooms.

Guests enjoy quiet evening walks, hiking, browsing in the antique shop or sitting by a peaceful creek.

INNKEEPERS: *Susyn Dragness*
ADDRESS: *7476 Highway 12*
  Morton, WA 98356
TELEPHONE: *(360) 498-5243; (800) 551-3290*
FAX: *Not Available*
EMAIL: *innkeeper@myhome.net*
WEBSITE: *Not Available*
ROOMS: *4 Rooms; Private and shared baths*
OPEN: *Year-round*
CHILDREN: *Children 10 and older are welcome*
ANIMALS: *Prohibited*
SMOKING: *Permitted in outside yard*

Baked Mini Pumpkins

Makes 1 serving, multiply as needed

These are as yummy as they are fun! Children and adults alike will be pleased to find one of these waiting for them at the table!

1 miniature pumpkin
1 tablespoon butter
2 tablespoons brown sugar
2 teaspoons chopped pecans, more or less
Maple syrup

PREHEAT OVEN TO 300°F. Wash and dry pumpkin. Cut out top and set aside. Clean out seeds. Put butter, brown sugar and pecans into pumpkin. Put top back on pumpkin. Place pumpkin in a baking pan and pour 1/4 cup water into bottom of pan. Bake for 40 minutes. Remove from oven and pour a little bit of maple syrup inside pumpkin. Put top back on and serve!

"My guests love these and they look so cute on the plates. They can be assembled the night before and baked in the morning."

Susyn Dragness - St. Helens Manorhouse

Carol's Corner

What fun stories you might hear at breakfast at this B & B, as Susyn, the innkeeper, claims St. Helens Manorhouse is haunted!

Annapurna Inn

L ocated in the Victorian seaport of Port Townsend, the Annapurna Inn is a retreat center that offers organic vegan cuisine, yoga, steam baths, saunas, foot reflexology, therapeutic massage and cranio/sacral therapy.

The delicious organic vegan breakfasts are planned around the philosophy and research of John McDougall, MD, Michael Klaper, MD, John Robbins and Dean Ornish, MD.

INNKEEPERS:	*Robin Sharan*
ADDRESS:	*538 Adams Street*
	Port Townsend, WA 98368
TELEPHONE:	*(360) 385-2909; (800) 868-2662*
FAX:	*(360) 379-0711*
EMAIL:	*annapurna@olympus.net*
WEBSITE:	*www.seattle2000.com*
ROOMS:	*6 Rooms; 1 Suite; 1 Cottage; Private and shared baths*
OPEN:	*Year-round*
CHILDREN:	*Welcome*
ANIMALS:	*Welcome; Resident cat*
SMOKING:	*Prohibited*

Tofu Scramble

Makes 6 servings

A nutritious vegan dish!

1 medium onion or leek, chopped
1/3 cup chopped celery
1 cup sliced mushrooms
1/3 cup sliced or chopped almonds
1 teaspoon sage
1 teaspoon turmeric
1/2 teaspoon marjoram
2 teaspoons tamari (soy sauce)
Salt, to taste
Pepper, to taste
1 pound firm tofu, mashed
1/4 cup chopped fresh cilantro

In a large skillet, sauté onion, celery, mushrooms and almonds with all of the seasonings. Add tofu, mix well and cook. Stir in cilantro and serve.

"We offer the very best in fabulous, fun, functional, friendly foods. Yeah!"

Robin Sharan - Annapurna Inn

🔖 Carol's Corner

A vegan [VEE-guhn; VEH-guhn] has the most limited diet of all vegetarians, avoiding consumption of any animal-derivative foods, including butter, cheese, eggs and milk.

Katy's Inn

N estled against a hillside, Katy's Inn Bed and Breakfast overlooks the Swinomish Channel in the old fishing village of LaConner. In 1876, Captain John Peck built this charming country Victorian home for his wife and four daughters.

Each of the five guest rooms is decorated with Victorian detail and comfort. All the rooms contain antiques and feather duvets.

INNKEEPERS:	*Bruce & Kathie Hubbard*
ADDRESS:	*503 South Third*
	LaConner, WA 98257
TELEPHONE:	*(360) 466-3366; (800) 914-7767*
FAX:	*(360) 466-1730*
EMAIL:	*katysinn@juno.com*
WEBSITE:	*www.pattismith.com/katys/*
ROOMS:	*4 Rooms; 1 Suite; Private and shared baths*
OPEN:	*Year-round*
CHILDREN:	*Children allowed in suite (Call ahead for guidelines)*
ANIMALS:	*Prohibited*
SMOKING:	*Permitted outside on porches or in yard*

Katy's Inn Rice Casserole

Makes 12 (1/2 cup) side-dish servings

4 tablespoons (1/2 stick) butter
1/2 cup chopped onion
1 cup sliced or slivered toasted almonds
1 (4 to 6-ounce) can mushrooms (or use fresh mushrooms)
2 (14 1/2-ounce) cans beef consommé
8 ounces (2 cups) grated cheddar cheese
1 3/4 cups uncooked instant rice

PREHEAT OVEN TO 325°F. In a small skillet, melt butter and sauté onion. In a casserole dish, mix sautéed onion with rest of ingredients. Bake, <u>covered</u>, for 1 hour and 15 minutes.

"I often double the recipe as the leftovers are great reheated (add a tablespoon or two of water if it gets too dry)."

Kathie Hubbard - Katy's Inn

Llama Ranch

N estled on 97 acres in a peaceful valley, the Llama Ranch Bed and Breakfast affords spectacular views of Mount St. Helens. Visitors enjoy the beauty of the valley and the serenity of walking with the llamas. Guests' llamas are boarded free.

Local activities include white water rafting, huckleberry picking, spelunking, windsurfing, hiking, cross-country skiing, fishing, biking and snowmobiling.

INNKEEPERS: *Jerry Stone*
ADDRESS: *1980 Highway 141*
                  Trout Lake, WA 98650
TELEPHONE: *(509) 395-2786*
FAX: *Not Available*
EMAIL: *lama1@linkport.com*
WEBSITE: *Not Available*
ROOMS: *6 Rooms; Private and shared baths*
OPEN: *Year-round*
CHILDREN: *Welcome*
ANIMALS: *Welcome (Dogs, cats, llamas)*
SMOKING: *Permitted outside only*

Rice Pudding

Makes 12 (2/3 cup) servings

The number of servings for this comforting pudding varies depending on whether it is used as a main breakfast dish or side dish. It may also be served as a dessert.

4 tablespoons butter
7 cups milk
1/2 cup sugar
1 cup short grain rice (such as Italian Arborio)
1 (8-inch) vanilla bean, split lengthwise (or 1 tablespoon vanilla extract)
2 cinnamon sticks (or 1/4 teaspoon ground cinnamon)
2 egg yolks
4 tablespoons water
1 (15-ounce) box (2 1/2 cups) golden raisins, soaked in hot water and drained

In a large saucepan, melt butter. Add milk, sugar, rice, vanilla bean halves with seeds (if using vanilla extract, stir in later when adding raisins) and cinnamon sticks. Bring to a boil and simmer for 8 minutes, stirring every 2 minutes. In a small bowl, combine egg yolks and water and stir into saucepan mixture. Simmer 10 minutes longer. Remove from heat. Remove and discard cinnamon sticks and vanilla bean halves. Add drained raisins (and vanilla extract, if using). Pour into a bowl and chill. Stir after 8-10 minutes and then again after another 8-10 minutes. Keep refrigerated until ready to serve. Note: This pudding may be served warm or cold.

> **Carol's Corner**
>
> *Using short-grain rice such as Italian Arborio gives the pudding an extra creamy texture; however, regular long-grain rice can be used and makes a delicious pudding as well.*

Cooney Mansion

T he Cooney Mansion Bed and Breakfast Inn was built in 1908 as the residence of lumber baron Neil Cooney, then manager of the Grays Harbor Commercial Company. This State and National Historic Register Landmark, with its abundance of fine woodwork, furniture and fixtures, has been restored to its original splendor.

A three-course "Lumber Baron's" breakfast is served at the massive original dining table.

INNKEEPERS:	*Judi & Jim Lohr*
ADDRESS:	*1705 Fifth Street*
	Cosmopolis, WA 98537
TELEPHONE:	*(360) 533-0602*
FAX:	*Not Available*
EMAIL:	*cooney@techline.com*
WEBSITE:	*www.techline.com/~cooney/*
ROOMS:	*5 Rooms; 1 Suite; All with private baths*
OPEN:	*Year-round*
CHILDREN:	*Children over 12 are welcome (Call for guidelines)*
ANIMALS:	*Prohibited*
SMOKING:	*Permitted outdoors only*

Santa Cruz Sweet and Sour Zucchini Salad

Makes 12 servings

Start this marinated salad a day ahead to allow full development of flavor.

3/4 cup sugar
1 teaspoon salt
1 teaspoon pepper
1/3 cup salad oil
2/3 cup cider vinegar
1/2 cup white wine vinegar
1 cup chopped green onions (about 10 medium onions)
8 cups <u>thinly</u> sliced zucchini (about 4-6 zucchini)
1/2 cup diced green pepper (about 1/2 medium pepper)
1/2 cup diced celery (1-2 ribs)

In a large bowl, combine sugar, salt, pepper, oil and vinegars. Add onions, zucchini, green pepper and celery. Mix well, cover and chill overnight. Drain well and serve.

Carol's Corner

The marinade for this salad is great! Vary this recipe by adding whatever you have in your garden—tomatoes, red peppers, cucumbers, yellow squash, etc.

Abendblume Pension

Luxurious accommodations surround guests of the Abendblume Pension Inn. The Schnesswittchen Room offers a private balcony, heated whirlpool tub, German fireplace and European linens and comforters.

Seasonal recreational activities include downhill and cross-country skiing, sleigh rides, sledding, river rafting, bicycling, alpine hiking, rock climbing, fishing and golfing.

INNKEEPERS:	*Randy & Renee Sexauer*
ADDRESS:	*12570 Ranger Road*
	Leavenworth, WA 98826
TELEPHONE:	*(509) 548-4059; (800) 669-7634*
FAX:	*(509) 548-9032*
EMAIL:	*abendblm@rightathome.com*
WEBSITE:	*www.abendblume.com*
ROOMS:	*7 Rooms; 4 Suites; All with private baths*
OPEN:	*Year-round*
CHILDREN:	*Prohibited*
ANIMALS:	*Prohibited*
SMOKING:	*Prohibited*

Spicy Cranberry-Orange Mold

Makes 10 servings

A nice accompaniment to Thanksgiving turkey!

1 1/2 cups ground fresh cranberries (<u>see substitution below</u>)
1/2 cup sugar (<u>see substitution below</u>)
1/4 teaspoon ground cinnamon
1/8 teaspoon ground cloves
1 large (6-ounce) package orange-flavored gelatin
1/4 teaspoon salt
2 cups boiling water
1 1/2 cups cold water (<u>see substitution below</u>)
1 tablespoon lemon juice
1 orange, peeled, sectioned and diced
1/2 cup chopped nuts or celery (or half of each)
Salad greens, for garnish (optional)

In a small bowl, combine cranberries, sugar, cinnamon and cloves. Set aside. In a large bowl, dissolve gelatin and salt in boiling water. Add cold water and lemon juice. Chill gelatin mixture until slightly thickened. Fold in cranberry mixture, orange, nuts or celery. Spoon into a 6-cup ring mold (or if you prefer, a 6-cup capacity serving bowl). Chill until firm, about 4 hours. Unmold. Garnish with salad greens, if desired.

<u>Substitution</u>: In place of fresh ground cranberries, you may use 1 can (16-ounce) whole berry cranberry sauce. Omit sugar and reduce cold water to 1 cup.

Carol's Corner

Try this refreshing salad using your favorite flavor of gelatin. My mother tried this recipe one day using what she had on hand (one 3-ounce package of apricot flavor and one 3-ounce package of mixed fruit flavor) and she reported that it was delicious!

Cooney Mansion

T he south lawn of the Cooney Mansion Bed and Breakfast Inn is framed by a rose garden laced with clematis, lilacs and peonies. The north lawn features a rhododendron grove and sprawling lawn surrounded by a pine forest.

Cooney Mansion hosts "A Dickens Family Christmas" the first two weeks in December, featuring high tea with Queen Victoria, arts and crafts and Victorian dinners.

INNKEEPERS:	*Judi & Jim Lohr*
ADDRESS:	*1705 Fifth Street*
	Cosmopolis, WA 98537
TELEPHONE:	*(360) 533-0602*
FAX:	*Not Available*
EMAIL:	*cooney@techline.com*
WEBSITE:	*www.techline.com/~cooney/*
ROOMS:	*5 Rooms; 1 Suite; All with private baths*
OPEN:	*Year-round*
CHILDREN:	*Children over 12 are welcome (Call for guidelines)*
ANIMALS:	*Prohibited*
SMOKING:	*Permitted outdoors only*

Judi's Chinese Chicken Salad

Makes 6 main-dish servings or 12 side-dish servings

Start this recipe several hours before serving. The marinated chicken adds great flavor to the salad!

2 tablespoons sugar
1 teaspoon salt
1 tablespoon vinegar
2 tablespoons soy sauce
1/4 teaspoon ground ginger
1 clove garlic, minced
1/2 cup salad oil
1/2 teaspoon white pepper
1/4 cup lemon juice
1 cup cooked and shredded chicken
1/2 head cabbage, shredded
1/2 head iceberg lettuce, shredded
1 bunch green onions, sliced
2 tablespoons toasted sesame seeds (toasted is better, but untoasted is fine)
2 tablespoons slivered almonds or chopped salted peanuts
1/2 package uncooked ramen noodles, crumbled
1/2 small bunch fresh cilantro, chopped

<u>To make dressing</u>: In a medium bowl, mix together sugar, salt, vinegar, soy sauce, ginger, garlic, oil, white pepper and lemon juice. Add cooked chicken, coating thoroughly with dressing, and allow to marinate in the refrigerator for several hours.

<u>Approximately 30 minutes before serving</u>: In a large bowl, mix together cabbage, lettuce, green onions, sesame seeds, almonds, ramen noodles and cilantro. Add chicken and dressing, toss together and serve.

Luncheon & Dinner Entrées

Luncheon & Dinner Entrées

Benson Farmstead

T he Benson Farmstead Bed and Breakfast is a cozy farmhouse that was lovingly restored in 1981 by Jerry and Sharon Benson, grandchildren of Skagit Valley Norwegian pioneers. This seventeen-room house is filled with lovely antiques, Scandinavian curios and old quilts.

"A little bit of heaven on earth."

~ Guest, Benson Farmstead

INNKEEPERS:	*Jerry & Sharon Benson*
ADDRESS:	*1009 Avon-Allen Road*
	Bow, WA 98232
TELEPHONE:	*(360) 757-0578; (800) 685-7239 (Pin: 1930)*
FAX:	*Not Available*
EMAIL:	*Not Available*
WEBSITE:	*www.bbhost.com/bensonbnb*
ROOMS:	*4 Rooms; All with private baths*
OPEN:	*Year-round (Weekends only Mid-September through March)*
CHILDREN:	*Welcome*
ANIMALS:	*Prohibited*
SMOKING:	*Prohibited*

Benson's Luncheon Chicken Casserole

Makes 8 servings

Great with cranberries, a salad and rolls!

7 chicken breasts
1 small onion, quartered
2 ribs celery, cut in several pieces
1 teaspoon Johnny's Pork & Chicken Seasoning (very flavorful
  seasoned salt)
1 (10 3/4-ounce) can cream of mushroom soup
1 pint sour cream
1/2 pound fresh mushrooms, sliced and sautéed
4 tablespoons (1/2 stick) margarine, melted
1 cup chicken stock (reserved from cooking chicken)
**1 (8-ounce) package Pepperidge Farm herb seasoned or cornbread
  stuffing mix**

Place chicken, onion and celery into a large saucepan; add enough water to cover. Cook gently for 30 minutes. Remove chicken and strain cooking liquid, <u>setting aside one cup</u> for later use in recipe. De-bone chicken and cut into chunks. PREHEAT OVEN TO 325°F. Coat a 13x9-inch baking dish with nonstick cooking spray. Place chicken in bottom of dish and sprinkle with seasoning. Cover with soup, add sour cream, then mushrooms. In a large bowl, combine melted margarine and chicken stock, then toss with stuffing mix and spread over top of ingredients in dish. Bake, uncovered, for 50 minutes.

Carol's Corner

In a hurry? Use boneless chicken breasts (they cook faster and it saves de-boning time) and substitute an 8-ounce can of mushrooms for the sautéed fresh ones.

7 C's Guest Ranch

T he 7 C's (Seven Seas) Guest Ranch Bed and Breakfast is a ten-acre farm that combines modern luxury with country comfort. After a peaceful night's rest, guests enjoy a delicious farm breakfast. Gourmet meals can be arranged in advance.

Special amenities include horseback riding, overnight stabling, hay rides or an outdoor hot spa that can accommodate seven.

INNKEEPERS:	*Evelyn B. Cissna*
ADDRESS:	*11123 128th SE*
	Rainier, WA 98576
TELEPHONE:	*(360) 446-7957*
FAX:	*Not Available*
EMAIL:	*Not Available*
WEBSITE:	*www.wolfe.net/~fin/bb/ (United States)*
	www.go-native.com/inns/0113.html (Europe)
ROOMS:	*4 Rooms; 1 Suite; Private and shared baths*
OPEN:	*Year-round*
CHILDREN:	*Welcome*
ANIMALS:	*Prohibited indoors; Permitted outdoors*
SMOKING:	*Permitted outside on covered porches and balconies*

Reception Turkey Salad

Makes 24 servings

This tasty salad is perfect for any occasion or celebration, from a neighborhood potluck or baby shower, to a wedding reception!

6 cups cubed cooked turkey or chicken
1 (8-ounce) can pineapple tidbits (<u>reserve juice</u>)
1 (11-ounce) can mandarin orange segments, drained
1 cup red or green grapes, halved
1 cup chopped apples
1 cup chopped celery
1/3 cup slivered or chopped sweet pickles
8 hard-cooked eggs, chopped
1 cup chopped cashews (<u>add just before serving</u>)

<u>**Dressing**</u>

2 cups Best Foods mayonnaise (don't substitute)
1/4 cup lemon juice
1/4 cup pineapple juice (from pineapple tidbits)
1 teaspoon grated lemon peel
2 teaspoons salt

In a very large bowl, mix together turkey (or chicken), pineapple, mandarin oranges, grapes, apples, celery, pickles and eggs. Set aside. <u>To make dressing</u>: In a medium bowl, combine mayonnaise, lemon juice, pineapple juice, lemon peel and salt. Pour over turkey/fruit mixture and stir to thoroughly combine. Refrigerate for several hours (if possible) to mingle the flavors. Add cashews just before serving.

<u>Make-ahead tip</u>: Salad may be made one day in advance, but remember to stir in cashews right before serving.

Moby Dick Hotel & Oyster Farm

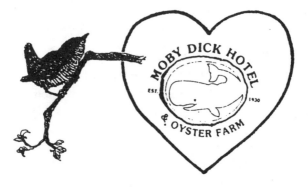

T he Moby Dick Hotel and Oyster Farm was originally built in 1929 as a hotel. During World War II, this historic dwelling was head-quarters to the United States Coast Guard Horse Patrol which patrolled the ocean beaches.

The spacious public rooms and rambling bay-front grounds provide an ideal setting for small focus groups, staff retreats or family reunions.

INNKEEPERS:	*Edward & Fritzi Cohen*
ADDRESS:	*Sandridge Road; PO Box 82*
	Nahcotta, WA 98637
TELEPHONE:	*(360) 665-4543*
FAX:	*(360) 665-6887*
EMAIL:	*mobydickhotel@willapabay.org*
WEBSITE:	*www.nwplace.com*
ROOMS:	*10 Rooms; Shared baths*
OPEN:	*Year-round*
CHILDREN:	*Welcome*
ANIMALS:	*Welcome (Dogs)*
SMOKING:	*Prohibited*

Moby Dick Oysters

Looking for an unusual and impressive appetizer? Here it is!

Oysters in the shell
Mustard greens, kale or arugula
Aioli (recipe to follow)
Parmesan cheese, grated

PREHEAT OVEN TO 500°F. OR TURN TO BROIL. Shuck or steam oysters open. Save shell halves that are the most attractive and stable. Finely chiffonade (cut into thin strips or shreds) the greens and put a bit into each shell. Put an oyster back into each shell on top of the greens. Put a bit of greens on top of each oyster. Top with a dab of aioli. Sprinkle with some Parmesan cheese and pop them in a very hot oven or under the broiler until the aioli browns very slightly.

Aioli

2 to 3 cloves of garlic, or more to taste
Handful of fresh herbs (basil and cilantro are good)
1 teaspoon salt
1 whole egg
1 egg yolk
Lemon or lime juice or various vinegars, to your taste (start with at least 1 generous tablespoon)
1 1/4 to 1 1/2 cups any high quality oil (Fritzi and Edward use a mix of olive and corn oils)

Into a food processor, put garlic, herbs and salt; blend. Add whole egg and one yolk, lemon or lime juice or vinegars and mix briefly. Then slowly dribble in oil (while processor is running) until mixture is thickened and of proper consistency. Keep any leftover aioli refrigerated.

> *"This is Moby Dick's version of Oysters Rockefeller. We serve it at dinner or as a garnish at breakfast with oyster breakfast dishes that we make."*
>
> *Fritzi and Edward Cohen - Moby Dick Hotel and Oyster Farm*

Carol's Corner

I didn't think I was a big oyster fan, but this recipe changed my mind! The oysters look beautiful atop their green "beds" and the garlic-flavored mayonnaise (aioli) is superb.

Selah Inn

Nestled on the north shore of the Hood Canal, Selah Inn on Dulalip Landing offers guests a memorable and relaxing experience. Dominating the living room of this elegant Northwest lodge is a magnificent rock fireplace. Amenities include luxurious bed linens, fresh flowers and chocolates.

Board room and conference facilities for small business meetings are available by prior arrangement. White board, overhead and computer hookups are provided.

INNKEEPERS:	*Pat & Bonnie McCullough*
ADDRESS:	*130 NE Dulalip Landing*
	Belfair, WA 98528
TELEPHONE:	*(360) 275-0916; (360) 275-0578*
FAX:	*(360) 277-3187*
EMAIL:	*esa@hctc.com*
WEBSITE:	*www.selahinn.com*
ROOMS:	*4 Rooms; 1 Suite; 2 Cottage; Private and shared baths*
OPEN:	*Year-round*
CHILDREN:	*Welcome (Cottages only)*
ANIMALS:	*Prohibited*
SMOKING:	*Permitted outdoors on covered porch*

Champagne Poached Oysters with Brie

Appetizers for 8 or entrées for 4

2 dozen clean oyster shells
1 (10-ounce) package chopped spinach, steamed and drained
1 cup champagne or sparkling wine
1/2 teaspoon saffron
1/2 teaspoon dried basil
1 pinch cayenne
1 quart shucked oysters (reserve oyster liquid)
1/2 cup sour cream
1/2 cup heavy cream
8 ounces Brie cheese, cut into 1-inch squares (rind removed)
Parsley, for garnish

PREHEAT OVEN TO 175°F. Fill each clean oyster shell with one tablespoon cooked spinach. Place shells on a baking sheet and "hold" in warm oven. In a large pan, simmer wine, saffron, basil and cayenne. Add oysters and reserved liquid. Poach oysters until plump and firm, about 3 minutes. With slotted spoon, remove oysters and place in individual shells. Hold in warm oven. Bring remaining liquid to a hard boil and reduce to 1/4 cup. Beat together sour cream and heavy cream. Stir into reduced liquid and heat until mixture begins to bubble. Add chunks of Brie. Whisk until cheese melts and sauce thickens. Pour over warm oysters, garnish with parsley and serve immediately.

Note: You may omit the oyster shells and spinach and serve the oysters with the sauce only.

The Captain Whidbey Inn

S ince 1907, The Captain Whidbey Inn has provided travelers with warm hospitality, wonderful food and comfortable rooms furnished with antiques, artwork, books, down comforters and feather beds.

Guests enjoy dining on world famous Penn Cove mussels, steelhead salmon, Dungeness crab or spot prawns, all provided by local fishermen to ensure peak freshness.

INNKEEPERS:	*Dennis Argent (Proprietor: John C. Stone)*
ADDRESS:	*2072 West Captain Whidbey Inn Road*
	Coupeville, Whidbey Island, WA 98239
TELEPHONE:	*(360) 678-4097; (800) 366-4097*
FAX:	*(360) 678-4110*
EMAIL:	*captain@whidbey.net*
WEBSITE:	*www.whidbey.net/~captain/*
ROOMS:	*25 Rooms; 7 Cabins; Shared baths*
OPEN:	*Year-round*
CHILDREN:	*Welcome*
ANIMALS:	*Prohibited*
SMOKING:	*Permitted in designated rooms*

Ginger Mussels

Makes 2 appetizer servings or 1 main-dish serving

A frequently requested recipe at The Captain Whidbey Inn!

1 pound mussels, cleaned and de-bearded (about 18-20 mussels per pound)
1 cup Ginger Mussel Mix (recipe to follow)

Place mussels into a hot sauté pan. Add Ginger Mussel Mix and cover. Cook until mussels open, about 3-5 minutes. (Discard any mussels that do not open.) Transfer mussels and broth to bowl and serve immediately.

Ginger Mussel Mix

Makes approximately 5 cups

3 tablespoons finely chopped fresh ginger
1 1/2 cups finely chopped scallions (about 3 bunches green onions)
3 garlic cloves, minced
1 tablespoon ground black pepper
5 jalapeño peppers, seeds and membranes removed, minced
1/4 cup sesame oil
1 1/8 cups rice vinegar
1/2 cup soy sauce
2 1/4 cups sake (Japanese rice wine)

Combine all ingredients. Store mixture in refrigerator. Stir and mix well before using.

Carol's Corner

Wash your hands thoroughly after removing the seeds and membranes from the jalapeño peppers (or wear rubber gloves). Otherwise, the juice and oils from the peppers can cause a burning sensation to your eyes if you accidentally touch them. If this should happen, flush your eyes immediately with water.

Chestnut Hill Inn

T he Chestnut Hill Inn Bed and Breakfast on Orcas Island offers the ultimate retreat in the grand country style. Nestled in a picturesque valley, this elegant estate provides the perfect setting for an extended summer adventure or a romantic winter retreat.

Amenities include cozy robes and slippers for snuggling by the fireplace, soaps, lotions, candies, stationery and apéritifs.

INNKEEPERS:	*Daniel & Marilyn Loewke*
ADDRESS:	*PO Box 213*
	Orcas, WA 98280
TELEPHONE:	*(360) 376-5157*
FAX:	*(360) 376-5283*
EMAIL:	*chestnut@pacificrim.net*
WEBSITE:	*www.chestnuthillinn.com*
ROOMS:	*4 Rooms; 1 Suite; 1 Cottage; All with private baths*
OPEN:	*Year-round*
CHILDREN:	*Children 13 and older are welcome (Call ahead)*
ANIMALS:	*Prohibited; Resident cats and a dog*
SMOKING:	*Prohibited*

Peppercorn-Crusted Salmon with White Wine Butter Sauce

Makes 4 servings

Salmon Marinade

1 1/2 cups water
1 cup light or dark brown sugar
3 tablespoons coarse salt, such as sea or kosher
1 tablespoon liquid smoke (located near the BBQ sauce in the grocery store)
1 tablespoon grated fresh ginger
3 bay leaves
1 teaspoon whole allspice
4 salmon fillets (about 2 pounds)
3 tablespoons cracked black peppercorns
2 tablespoons + 2 teaspoons honey

White Wine Butter Sauce

1 cup dry white wine
1 shallot, minced
2 tablespoons vinegar, preferably white wine
1/2 cup heavy cream
6 tablespoons cold, firm butter
1 pinch fresh dill
4 sprigs fresh dill, for garnish (optional)

In a medium saucepan, combine water, brown sugar, salt, liquid smoke, ginger, bay leaves and allspice. Bring to boil. Reduce heat and simmer until sugar is dissolved, about 5 minutes. Remove from heat and cool at least 15 minutes. Place salmon in glass baking dish. Pour marinade over salmon. Cover and refrigerate for 6 hours, or overnight, turning salmon occasionally. Line a baking sheet with parchment paper. Remove salmon from marinade, reserving marinade. Pat fillets dry with paper towels. Place fillets skin-side down on baking sheet. Strain reserved marinade into a saucepan; discard solids. Add peppercorns. Bring to boil. Reduce heat; simmer for 10 minutes. Strain, reserving pepper; discard liquid. Spread honey over tops of salmon; sprinkle with peppercorns. PREHEAT OVEN TO 350°F. Bake for 20-25 minutes or until fish flakes easily. While oven is preheating, start making sauce. It will take 25 minutes. Don't try to skimp on cooking time or the sauce will not be thick enough. In a small saucepan, combine wine, shallots and vinegar. Bring to boil. Cook until syrupy and reduced to 2 tablespoons, about 10 minutes. Add cream; bring to boil. Cook until reduced by half (about 1/4 cup), about 8 minutes. Strain sauce and return to saucepan. Bring to boil and remove from heat. Add butter (1 tablespoon at a time), whisking until each addition is melted and smooth. Add pinch of fresh dill.

To serve: On each plate, pour a circle of sauce and place a fillet over sauce. Using a zigzag motion, drizzle small amount of sauce over each fillet. Garnish with sprig of fresh dill.

Inn at Barnum Point

The Inn at Barnum Point is a birdwatcher's haven. Guests observe magnificent soaring eagles, diminutive hummingbirds, flocks of Dunlin or happy goldfinch munching on cherries.

Animal lovers discover seals and otters playing in the water, deer grazing in the orchard or hear coyotes howling in the night.

INNKEEPERS:	*Carolin Barnum Dilorenzo*
ADDRESS:	*464 South Barnum Road*
	Camano Island, WA 98292
TELEPHONE:	*(360) 387-2256; (800) 910-2256*
FAX:	*(360) 387-2256*
EMAIL:	*Not Available*
WEBSITE:	*www.whidbey.com/inn/*
ROOMS:	*2 Rooms; Private baths*
OPEN:	*Year-round*
CHILDREN:	*Welcome*
ANIMALS:	*Prohibited*
SMOKING:	*Prohibited*

Salmon with Blackberry Sauce

Makes 4 servings

2 cups blackberries, divided (if frozen, thaw before using)
1/4 cup sugar
1/4 cup water
1/4 cup red wine vinegar
1/2 tablespoon butter
1/4 cup minced onions or shallots
1/4 cup dry red wine
Salt and pepper, to taste
4 salmon fillets, about 1/2 pound each, skinned
1/4 teaspoon ground cloves
3 tablespoons fresh thyme leaves (a few sprigs are OK)
1 1/2 tablespoons salad oil

In a food processor or blender, purée 1 1/2 cups blackberries. Pass berries through a fine sieve, using back of spoon to help push purée through. Discard seeds. Set aside berry purée. In a small saucepan, mix sugar with water. Cook uncovered over medium-high heat until reduced to a thick, light caramel colored syrup (about 5-10 minutes). Remove from heat; add vinegar. Return to low heat and stir until thick caramel syrup is thoroughly combined with the vinegar. Pour into a dish and set aside. Rinse pan. In same pan, melt butter over medium-high heat and add onions. Cook, stirring often, until just golden brown (about 2-3 minutes). Add wine and cook uncovered until most of liquid evaporates (about 5-10 minutes, watch carefully). Add berry purée and cook uncovered until reduced by half (about 6-10 minutes). Add half of vinegar/sugar/water mixture (or more to taste) that you set aside. Add salt and pepper to taste. Set aside. Rinse fish; pat dry. Salt and pepper to taste. Sprinkle cloves on plate and sprinkle thyme over it. Put salmon fillets on top, turning to coat each side. PREHEAT OVEN TO 375°F. Add oil to 10 or 12-inch ovenproof skillet. Over high heat, cook fish until lightly browned, 1-2 minutes per side. Transfer to preheated oven and bake 4-6 minutes or until barely opaque in thickest part. (Cut fish to test.) While salmon cooks, add remaining whole blackberries to sauce and heat on medium until heated through (3-4 minutes).

To serve: Divide sauce by spooning onto 4 serving plates and place a salmon fillet on top, using the whole berries as garnish. Add sprig of thyme to finish presentation.

Make-ahead tip: Make blackberry sauce the day before serving. Reheat sauce while salmon is cooking.

Selah Inn

T he spectacular Northwest wonderland of the Hood Canal awaits guests of the Selah Inn. The Hood Canal, a 60-mile extension of Puget Sound, is a haven for wildlife. Beach walks are a great opportunity to observe eagles, cranes, gulls, ducks and sea lions.

McCormick Woods and Gold Mountain golf courses are within 10 miles of the inn. Bike trails and off-road recreational vehicle trails abound in a local off-road recreational park.

INNKEEPERS:	*Pat & Bonnie McCullough*
ADDRESS:	*130 NE Dulalip Landing*
	Belfair, WA 98528
TELEPHONE:	*(360) 275-0916; (360) 275-0578*
FAX:	*(360) 277-3187*
EMAIL:	*esa@hctc.com*
WEBSITE:	*www.selahinn.com*
ROOMS:	*4 Rooms; 1 Suite; 2 Cottage; Private and shared baths*
OPEN:	*Year-round*
CHILDREN:	*Welcome (Cottages only)*
ANIMALS:	*Prohibited*
SMOKING:	*Permitted outdoors on covered porch*

Salmon with Roasted Garlic and Sun-Dried Tomato Herb Butter

Makes 4 servings

1 bulb garlic, roasted (directions below)
4 tablespoons olive oil, divided
1/3 cup sun-dried tomatoes (soaked in water, drained) or sun-dried
  tomatoes packed in oil (drained)
1/2 cup (1 stick) butter
1 teaspoon dried rosemary
2 pounds boneless, skinless salmon fillet
Old Bay seasoning (for seafood, poultry and meats)
Fresh dill, for garnish
Lemon wedges, for garnish

To roast garlic: PREHEAT OVEN TO 350°F. With a sharp knife, cut about 1/4-inch off top of bulb. (Leave paperlike skin on to hold cloves together.) On a small sheet of foil, pour one tablespoon of olive oil. Place garlic bulb cut-side down on oil; wrap foil around bulb. Bake for 45-60 minutes. Unwrap garlic. Cool, then gently squeeze garlic "paste" out of cloves and into bowl of food processor.

To make herb butter: In a food processor, blend together roasted garlic, 3 tablespoons olive oil, sun-dried tomatoes, butter and rosemary. (Make-ahead tip: This may be made in advance and stored in refrigerator until one hour before using.)

To cook salmon: PREHEAT OVEN TO 425°F. Cover a baking sheet with ungreased foil. Rinse salmon with cold water, pat dry with paper towels and lay on foil-covered pan. Sprinkle fillet with Old Bay seasoning. Spread herb butter mixture evenly over top of salmon. Bake 10-12 minutes, checking occasionally for doneness by inserting a knife or fork into the thickest part and gently parting the flesh. Fish is done when just opaque throughout; do not overcook. Slice into serving portions. Serve at once garnished with fresh dill and lemon wedges.

The Captain Whidbey Inn

I nnkeeper John Colby Stone is a sailing charter captain. Guests of The Captain Whidbey Inn often book an afternoon on his fifty-two foot classic wooden ketch, *Cutty Sark*. Captain Stone encourages his guests to take a turn at the helm, help trim the sails or simply enjoy the cruise with its splendid views of the water, islands and mountains.

The Inn's charming dining room overlooks the beautiful waters of Penn Cove.

INNKEEPERS:	*Dennis Argent (Proprietor: John C. Stone)*
ADDRESS:	*2072 West Captain Whidbey Inn Road*
	Coupeville, Whidbey Island, WA 98239
TELEPHONE:	*(360) 678-4097; (800) 366-4097*
FAX:	*(360) 678-4110*
EMAIL:	*captain@whidbey.net*
WEBSITE:	*www.whidbey.net/~captain/*
ROOMS:	*25 Rooms; 7 Cabins; Shared baths*
OPEN:	*Year-round*
CHILDREN:	*Welcome*
ANIMALS:	*Prohibited*
SMOKING:	*Permitted in designated rooms*

Sesame-Crusted Halibut with Lemon Sage Butter

Makes 4 servings

1 cup sesame seeds
1/2 cup flour
Salt, to taste
White pepper, to taste
1/2 cup milk, approximately
4 halibut fillets (about 4 ounces each)
2 to 3 tablespoons olive oil
Wood plank for baking fish (see note below from chef)
Lemon sage butter (recipe to follow)

PREHEAT OVEN TO 425°F. In a small shallow pan (or on waxed paper), mix together sesame seeds, flour, salt and white pepper. Into another small shallow pan or bowl, pour milk. First dip fish into milk; then dip fillets into sesame seed/flour mixture, turning to give each side a light coating. Using two medium nonstick sauté pans, heat oil on high and bring it to a smoke. Add two fillets for each pan and brown each side, about 1 minute each side. Place fish on wood plank and bake in oven about 10-15 minutes, or until flesh feels firm to the touch. Place each fillet on a serving plate and top each one with a tablespoon of lemon sage butter.

Lemon Sage Butter

Makes one (12-14-inch) log, enough for 32 servings

This herb butter is delicious and a great accompaniment to the fish. The recipe makes a lot, but can easily be reduced, or freeze the extra for later use.

1 pound butter, room temperature
2 tablespoons chopped fresh sage leaves
2 tablespoons minced garlic
Juice and grated zest (peel) of 1 lemon

In a medium bowl, mix together all ingredients with an electric mixer and whip until fluffy. Shape into a 12-14-inch log and wrap in waxed paper. Chill until butter is firm.

> *"Native Americans used wood to barbecue fish on open fire pits.*
> *It flavors the halibut with a hint of charred wood and helps keep the flesh*
> *tender. Untreated alder, hickory, cherry or cedar planks work well."*
>
> *Sam Chapman, Executive Chef - The Captain Whidbey Inn*

Carol's Corner
Beautiful wood planks designed for baking can be found at kitchen stores, or less expensive rustic boards can be purchased at home improvement or lumber stores.

Ann Starrett Mansion

A national historic landmark
1889

Internationally renowned for its classic Victorian architecture, the Ann Starrett Mansion features frescoed ceilings and a free hung, three-tiered spiral staircase that leads to one of the most unusual domed ceilings in North America. The eight-sided dome is actually a glorified solar calendar with frescoes depicting the four seasons and four virtues.

The interior is exquisitely detailed with moldings that feature carved lions, doves and ferns.

INNKEEPERS:	*Edel Sokol*
ADDRESS:	*744 Clay Street*
	Port Townsend, WA 98368
TELEPHONE:	*(360) 385-3250; (800) 321-0644*
FAX:	*(360) 385-2976*
EMAIL:	*Not Available*
WEBSITE:	*www.olympus.net/starrett*
ROOMS:	*7 Rooms; 4 Suites; 2 Cottages; Private baths*
OPEN:	*Year-round*
CHILDREN:	*Children under 12 are welcome (Cottages only)*
ANIMALS:	*Prohibited*
SMOKING:	*Prohibited*

Veal Escalopes with Mussels

Makes 4 servings

Fresh vegetables and pasta are nice accompaniments.

6 tablespoons butter, divided
20 cooked mussels, shelled
4 veal escalopes (4 to 5-ounces each)
Salt, to taste
1/2 cup white wine (do not use cooking wine as it is too salty)
4 tablespoons light cream
Sprigs of fresh fennel or dill, for garnish

In a large skillet, melt 2 tablespoons butter and fry mussels. Remove and keep warm by covering with foil. Save juices in skillet. In another large skillet, melt 2 tablespoons of butter and fry the veal over high heat until golden, seasoning with a little salt. (Do not overcook as that toughens the meat.) Remove veal from skillet and keep warm with mussels. Add the juices from mussels to the skillet containing veal juices and add wine. Boil about 2 minutes, stirring while adding cream and remaining 2 tablespoons of butter; combine thoroughly. Lay veal and mussels on a warmed serving dish and top with sauce. Garnish with fennel or dill.

Carol's Corner

Escalope is a French term for a very thin, usually flattened, slice of meat. This recipe also works well using pork loin or chicken (pound it thin). Cook meat briefly so it remains tender.

The Manor Farm Inn

The Manor Farm Inn offers guests an oasis of tranquillity and seclusion. Its 25 pastoral acres boast a century-old farmhouse, porches and verandah posts framed by delicate climbing rose vines and a happy profusion of seasonal flowers.

The decor is unpretentiously lovely with country French pine antiques, colorful flower baskets and cozy firelit nooks.

INNKEEPERS:	*Jill & Don Day*
ADDRESS:	*26069 Big Valley Road NE*
	Poulsbo, WA 98370
TELEPHONE:	*(360) 779-4628*
FAX:	*(360) 779-4876*
EMAIL:	*office@manorfarminn.com*
WEBSITE:	*www.manorfarminn.com*
ROOMS:	*7 Rooms; All with private baths*
OPEN:	*Year-round*
CHILDREN:	*Children over 16 are welcome*
ANIMALS:	*Prohibited*
SMOKING:	*Permitted outside only*

Balsamic and Beer-Braised Lamb with Rosemary White Beans

Makes 4-6 servings

Ask your butcher to cut the meat off the bone and into cubes. Save the bone, as it will add flavor to the beans. Remember to start this recipe the day before, as the beans need to soak overnight. If you are short of time, substitute with 2 or 3 cans of white beans. Just add seasonings and heat.

Beans

1 1/2 cups white beans, soaked in water overnight and drained
2 (14 1/2-ounce) cans vegetable broth
1 lamb bone (optional)
Salt, to taste
Pepper, to taste
1 1/2 teaspoons chopped fresh rosemary
1 head garlic, roasted (see Carol's Corner)

In a large pot, cover soaked and drained beans with vegetable broth. (Add lamb bone, if desired.) Bring to a boil, cover, lower heat and simmer until tender (about 1 hour). Season with salt, pepper and rosemary. Squeeze roasted garlic cloves into beans and mix gently. Keep warm until ready to serve.

Lamb

3 tablespoons olive oil, divided
2 pounds leg of lamb, cut into 1-inch cubes
1 small onion, thinly sliced
1 (12-ounce) bottle beer (ale)
1 cup balsamic vinegar
1 cup stock (preferably lamb)
Cornstarch slurry (mix 2 tablespoons cornstarch with 2 tablespoons water)

In a large skillet over high heat, add approximately 2 tablespoons olive oil and sear lamb in small batches, browning evenly. Remove lamb and set aside. Add additional oil to skillet and slowly, lightly brown onions. Return lamb to pan. Deglaze pan with beer and add vinegar and stock. Bring to a simmer and cover. Let lamb cook gently for 1 to 1 1/2 hours or until tender. Add cornstarch slurry and stir until thickened. Serve over or around the beans.

 Carol's Corner

A head of garlic is also sometimes called a bulb. It is made up of sections called cloves. To roast garlic, see page 225.

The Willows Inn

S et against a backdrop of colorful rhododendrons and towering evergreens, The Willows Inn Bed and Breakfast is an island retreat where guests enjoy spectacular sunsets over the Gulf Islands. Situated on Lummi, this wooded, rural island is graced with tranquil beaches and 18 miles of country roads ideal for biking, bird watching or hiking.

The inn offers complete wedding services, including ceremony, reception and honeymoon.

INNKEEPERS:	*Victoria & Gary Flynn*
ADDRESS:	*2579 West Shore Drive*
	Lummi Island, WA 98262
TELEPHONE:	*(360) 758-2620*
FAX:	*Not Available*
EMAIL:	*willows@pacificrim.net*
WEBSITE:	*www.pacificrim.net/~willows*
ROOMS:	*7 Rooms; 2 Suites; 1 Cottage; All with private baths*
OPEN:	*Year-round*
CHILDREN:	*Children over 8 are welcome (Cottage & guest house only)*
ANIMALS:	*Prohibited*
SMOKING:	*Permitted outdoors only*

Victoria's Herbed Lamb Chops

Makes 1 serving (multiply as needed for each additional person)

Ellensburg lamb chops come from a quaint college town in Central Washington known for its tender succulent lamb. This recipe is easy and elegant, but you do have to plan ahead.

2 thick double Ellensburg lamb chops
1 tablespoon chopped fresh rosemary
1 tablespoon chopped fresh thyme
1 tablespoon chopped fresh sage
1 tablespoon dried Italian seasoning
2 garlic cloves, minced
Olive oil
3 fresh rosemary branches

Twenty-four hours ahead, trim all fat from lamb chops. In a small bowl, make dry marinade by mixing together rosemary, thyme, sage, Italian seasoning and garlic. Lightly coat a glass dish or pan with olive oil and sprinkle in some of the herb mixture. Place chops on mixture and rub with more olive oil and herbs. Place a couple rosemary branches on top, cover and refrigerate overnight. Prior to cooking, bring lamb chops to room temperature. PREHEAT GRILL. Grill the chops 4 minutes on first side and 3 minutes on other side, or to desired doneness. (Lamb may be served medium-rare; be careful not to overcook.) Turn off grill and allow chops to rest for a couple of minutes, or remove and rest chops on warm plate. Garnish with a fresh rosemary branch.

Carol's Corner

This special recipe was served at a winemaker's dinner featuring the Chinook Winery in November 1994. Victoria Flynn and her husband Gary, a wine connoisseur, both innkeepers at The Willows Inn, suggest the following accompaniments when serving lamb chops: minted and buttered tiny red potatoes, honeyed baby carrots, steamed asparagus topped with chopped toasted hazelnuts and a bottle of Chinook Merlot.

A Touch of Europe

S ituated on an acre of maple, pine, birch, cedar and spruce trees and surrounded by an array of beautiful flowers, A Touch of Europe Bed and Breakfast Inn invites guests to enjoy a true Victorian atmosphere enriched with old-world European charm and hospitality.

Guests complement their stay by visiting local wineries, antique shops, museums, or strolling, biking and jogging along Yakima's Greenway Path.

INNKEEPERS:	*Erika G. & James A. Cenci*
ADDRESS:	*220 North 16th Avenue*
	Yakima, WA 98902
TELEPHONE:	*(509) 454-9775; (888) 438-7073*
FAX:	*Not Available*
EMAIL:	*Not Available*
WEBSITE:	*www.winesnw.com/toucheuropeb&b.htm*
ROOMS:	*3 Rooms; All with private baths*
OPEN:	*Year-round*
CHILDREN:	*Prohibited*
ANIMALS:	*Prohibited*
SMOKING:	*Permitted outside only*

Signature Medallions of Pork Tenderloin in a Pink Peppercorn-Riesling Sauce

Makes 4-6 servings

2 tablespoons unsalted butter
1 teaspoon olive oil
1 1/2 to 2 pounds pork tenderloin, cut into 1/2-inch slices
2 shallots, peeled and chopped
Sea salt, to taste
Black pepper, to taste
1/2 cup dry Riesling wine
1 cup heavy cream
1 teaspoon whole pink peppercorns
1/2 cup sour cream
1 tablespoon chopped parsley, for garnish

In a medium skillet, heat butter and oil and brown pork slices in small batches. Remove as they are ready and keep them warm by covering with foil. In same pan, cook shallots gently until soft. Return meat to pan and add salt and pepper. Stir in wine; cook for 5 minutes. Stir in cream and simmer 15 more minutes. Add pink peppercorns and sour cream. Stir over low heat until sauce is smooth. Place several medallions on each serving plate. Top with a spoonful of sauce, and garnish with parsley.

Carol's Corner

The pink peppercorns in this delightful sauce add not only flavor but also a colorful touch. Pink peppercorns are not true peppercorns but actually freeze-dried berries from a rose plant cultivated in Madagascar. The berries are pungent and slightly sweet and can usually be found in gourmet stores.

Mountain Home Lodge

S ecluded in its own alpine valley, Mountain Home Lodge overlooks a
20-acre meadow with the grandeur of the Stuart Range in the
background. This sheltered hideaway offers one of the Northwest's
most spectacular settings for relaxation and adventure.

During winter, access to this private lodge is provided by tracked
Snowcats. Guests enjoy cross-country skiing, snowmobiling or
frolicking on the 1700-foot sledding hill.

INNKEEPERS:	*Brad & Kathy Schmidt*
ADDRESS:	*8201 Mountain Home Road*
	Leavenworth, WA 98826
TELEPHONE:	*(509) 548-7077; (800) 414-2378*
FAX:	*(509) 548-5008*
EMAIL:	*info@mthome.com*
WEBSITE:	*www.mthome.com*
ROOMS:	*9 Rooms; 1 Suite; 1 Cabin; All with private baths*
OPEN:	*Year-round*
CHILDREN:	*Specific guidelines for children (Call ahead)*
ANIMALS:	*Prohibited*
SMOKING:	*Prohibited*

Duck with Marionberry Compote

A delicious Northwest berry sauce to serve with duck or chicken. Plan ahead for this one as the poultry marinates for 1 to 2 hours and then cooks for 2 hours in a smoker. Home smokers are very popular these days and can be purchased at most major discount chains and wholesale clubs, as well as cookware and hardware stores.

1 cup soy sauce
1 cup sugar
1 teaspoon ground ginger
1 teaspoon minced garlic
4 cups water
Boneless duck breasts (or chicken)
Marionberry Compote (recipe to follow)

In a large bowl, combine soy sauce, sugar, ginger, garlic and water. Stir to thoroughly combine. Add duck or chicken breasts and marinate for 1-2 hours in refrigerator. Remove meat from marinade (discard marinade) and smoke meat for about 2 hours, adjusting length of time to your particular smoker. Slice meat thinly on the diagonal. Serve with marionberry compote.

Marionberry Compote

Makes 2 cups (enough for 6-8 servings)

2 cups marionberries (or other blackberries)
1 teaspoon ground cinnamon
2 cups sugar
1/3 cup balsamic vinegar

In a large saucepan, combine berries, cinnamon, sugar and vinegar. Cook over medium-low heat until thickened, approximately 2 hours. Set aside to cool slightly (it will thicken a bit). Sauce should be served warm. Presentation of compote can be under the meat or designed alongside.

Make-ahead tip: Compote can be made a day or two in advance and refrigerated. Reheat on stovetop or microwave. Thin with a little water, if necessary.

B & B Potpourri

B & B
Potpourri

Island Escape

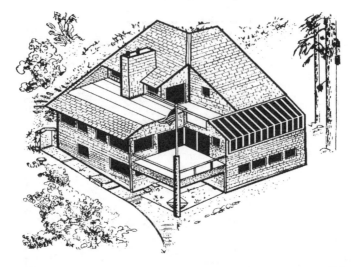

Recessed lighting sets the tone for a romantic getaway at Island Escape Bed and Breakfast. This singular suite features a private entrance, deck, garden area and a hammock-built-for-two with spectacular views of the Olympic Mountains.

Amenities include fresh flowers, bedside chocolates, fluffy towels and robes, herbal bath grains, oatmeal shell hand soaps and a bottle of sparkling cider upon arrival.

INNKEEPERS:	*Paula E. Pascoe*
ADDRESS:	*210 Island Boulevard*
	Fox Island, WA 98333
TELEPHONE:	*(253) 549-2044*
FAX:	*Not Available*
EMAIL:	*islandescape@narrows.com*
WEBSITE:	*www.narrows.com/islandescape*
ROOMS:	*1 Suite; Private bath*
OPEN:	*Year-round*
CHILDREN:	*Welcome*
ANIMALS:	*Prohibited*
SMOKING:	*Prohibited*

Island Escape's Popular Orange Smoothies

Makes about 3 cups (2-4 servings)

2 cups orange juice
1/2 cup plain nonfat yogurt
2 tablespoons sugar
1 cup crushed ice
Fresh mint sprigs, for garnish

In a blender, mix together all of the above ingredients (except mint). Serve in pre-chilled glasses. Top with your favorite mint sprig. (Paula rotates between her backyard mints: orange, apple and chocolate.)

> *"I freeze peeled bananas cut into chunks in plastic freezer bags; they hold for nearly two weeks without turning brown. To make the orange smoothie heartier during winter months, I add three or four chunks of frozen banana to my smoothies. The frozen chunks slice easily and I only add a slice at a time so that it blends well with the rest of the mixture."*
>
> *Paula Pascoe - Island Escape*

Run of the River

R un of the River Bed and Breakfast is the perfect getaway to enjoy mountains, streams, wildflowers and waterfalls. This natural log lodging features expansive views of the spectacular Icicle River and the Cascade Mountains.

Guest rooms offer hand-hewn log furniture, spacious decks and easy access to the hot tub that overlooks the river.

INNKEEPERS:	*Monty & Karen Turner*
ADDRESS:	*9308 E. Leavenworth Road*
	Leavenworth, WA 98826
TELEPHONE:	*(509) 548-7171; (800) 288-6491*
FAX:	*(509) 548-7547*
EMAIL:	*rother@rightathome.com*
WEBSITE:	*www.runoftheriver.com*
ROOMS:	*6 Rooms; All with private baths*
OPEN:	*Year-round*
CHILDREN:	*Prohibited*
ANIMALS:	*Prohibited*
SMOKING:	*Prohibited*

Boat Drinks

All recipes make 6 cups (see next page for <u>more</u> Boat Drinks)

"The following boat drinks from Run of the River can be added to or altered to suit individual needs. As you can see, the secret is to use the freshest local ingredients. In season, the blueberry, raspberry, strawberry and peach smoothies are wonderful. In the fall, winter and spring, we serve Pure Gold [using Golden Delicious Apples]. Guests enjoy the fresh tastes of Washington and Wenatchee Valley. Boat drinks are the most 'asked for' breakfast recipe we serve at the inn. Maybe we should change the menu? 'Boat drinks' is a take-off from a Jimmy Buffett tune. You don't have to love Buffett to enjoy these drinks, but it helps."

Monty Turner - Run of the River

Razzmatazz

2 cups raspberries
1 1/2 cups raspberry yogurt
1 banana
1 tablespoon wheat bran
3 cups Woodring Orchards Apple Cider

Whirl all ingredients in blender until smooth.

Blue Wave

2 cups blueberries
1 1/2 cups blueberry yogurt
1 banana
2 tablespoons molasses
3 cups Woodring Orchards Apple Cider
1 tablespoon flax seeds (available at health food stores)

Whirl all ingredients in blender until smooth.

Carol's Corner

Woodring Orchards Apple Cider is a non-pasteurized cider made in Cashmere, Washington. It is available at fruit stands throughout the valley and at Pike Place Market in Seattle. If this cider is not available in your area, substitute any good "country style" unfiltered cider.

Run of the River

S et in Washington's Cascade Range, Run of the River Bed and Breakfast offers guests a chance to connect with nature and experience the simple beauty of four seasons in the country.

"People who come here like to hike and bike and explore. They come for sun-filled, mountain-filled days. It's a beautiful place where you can do nothing but sit and read. It's also a wonderful area for getting out and connecting with nature."

~ Owners, Run of the River

INNKEEPERS:	*Monty & Karen Turner*
ADDRESS:	*9308 E. Leavenworth Road*
	Leavenworth, WA 98826
TELEPHONE:	*(509) 548-7171; (800) 288-6491*
FAX:	*(509) 548-7547*
EMAIL:	*rother@rightathome.com*
WEBSITE:	*www.runoftheriver.com*
ROOMS:	*6 Rooms; All with private baths*
OPEN:	*Year-round*
CHILDREN:	*Prohibited*
ANIMALS:	*Prohibited*
SMOKING:	*Prohibited*

More Boat Drinks!

These breakfast smoothies are not only great tasting, but they are also good for you! The yogurt in them (Run of the River uses low or nonfat) raises the calcium and protein content, and the bran, seeds, and fruit increase your intake of fiber. Drink up!

Pure Gold

1 large Golden Delicious apple, cored and cubed (OK to leave skin on)
1 banana
1 tablespoon chopped almonds
1 1/2 cups vanilla yogurt
3 cups Woodring Orchards Apple Cider

Whirl all ingredients in blender until smooth.

The Berries and the Bees

2 cups strawberries
1 banana
1 tablespoon bee pollen (available at health food stores)
1 1/2 cups strawberry yogurt
3 cups Woodring Orchards Apple Cider

Whirl all ingredients in blender until smooth.

You're A Peach

2 medium pitted peaches (leave skins on)
1 banana
1 tablespoon chopped pecans
1 1/2 cups of peach yogurt
3 cups Woodring Orchards Apple Cider

Whirl all ingredients in blender until smooth.

Carol's Corner

Rod and I, along with our friends Terri and Ken, were served a Berries and the Bees Boat Drink at Run of the River. The delicious drink gave us the energy to try snowshoeing for the very first time! Run of the River offers complimentary snowshoes for their guests' enjoyment. It was a lot of fun, as well as great exercise!

Country Inn Guest House

L ocated on a working farm and cattle ranch in the Palouse Hills of eastern Washington State, the Country Inn Guest House is less than a mile from the old Milwaukee Railroad Corridor, also known as the John Wayne Trail.

Innkeeper Kent is a third generation owner of this 100-year-old homestead. Innkeeper Jeanne gives historical tours that include the oldest consecrated church in Washington.

INNKEEPERS:	*Kent & Jeanne Kjack*
ADDRESS:	*1402 Cache Creek Road*
	Rosalia, WA 99170
TELEPHONE:	*(509) 569-3312*
FAX:	*Not Available*
EMAIL:	*Not Available*
WEBSITE:	*www.bnbweb.com/country-inn.html*
ROOMS:	*1 Room; 1 Suite; 1 Cottage; All with private baths*
OPEN:	*April through November*
CHILDREN:	*Welcome*
ANIMALS:	*Welcome (Domestic pets must be on a leash)*
SMOKING:	*Permitted outside only*

Smoked Salmon Roll-Ups

Makes 12-14 logs (approximately 50-60 bite-size appetizers)

1/2 pound smoked salmon, flaked or mashed with a fork (remove any bones first)
Mayonnaise (enough to stick the salmon together)
1 tablespoon celery, finely chopped
1 tablespoon onion, finely chopped
1/2 teaspoon garlic powder
Salt, to taste
1 (8-ounce) package cream cheese, room temperature
Approximately 14-16 slices fresh white bread

In a small bowl, mix salmon and mayonnaise together. Add celery, onion and garlic powder. Thoroughly mix. Taste for salt. Most smoked fish has enough, but if you need to, add some salt at this point. Add more mayonnaise (or a little sour cream) until a nice consistency is reached. (Sour cream will add moisture without mayonnaise taste.) Trim off crusts of bread. Roll each slice flat with a rolling pin. Spread each slice with cream cheese. Then spread each slice with some salmon mixture. Roll each slice up into a log. Cut each log into 4 or 5 chunks. Cover and refrigerate until serving time. Skewer with cocktail toothpicks.

Serving suggestion: Place roll-ups on a tray with an assortment of cheese cubes and fruit.

Smoked Salmon Pâté

Use the same ingredients as Smoked Salmon Roll-ups, except omit cream cheese and bread.

Mix all ingredients together and place in a small serving bowl. Serve with a variety of crackers.

"I have made these salmon logs ahead, frozen them in plastic bags, thawed and then sliced them for guests. I even fixed these for our son's wedding and froze them 5 days ahead! For the pâté, any smoked fish can be used, but I think salmon is best."

Jeanne Kjack - Country Inn Guest Ranch

Beachside

Beachside Bed and Breakfast is the perfect getaway for a romantic overnight or a special vacation. From the chintz-covered furniture to the flower gardens on the private patio, guests are surrounded by the ambiance of a traditional English cottage.

Amenities include a fully-equipped kitchen, woodburning fireplace, large hot tub, an extended continental breakfast and a deep moorage buoy for boaters.

INNKEEPERS:	*Doreen & Dick Samuelson*
ADDRESS:	*679 Kamus Drive*
	Fox Island, WA 98333
TELEPHONE:	*(253) 549-2524*
FAX:	*Not Available*
EMAIL:	*Not Available*
WEBSITE:	*Not Available*
ROOMS:	*1 Suite; Private bath*
OPEN:	*Year-round*
CHILDREN:	*Welcome*
ANIMALS:	*Prohibited*
SMOKING:	*Prohibited*

Crabby Cheese Muffins

Makes 12 muffin halves or 48 appetizers

6 English muffins
1/2 cup (1 stick) butter or margarine, room temperature (the amount may be cut back a little, if desired)
1 (5-ounce) jar Old English cheese
1/2 teaspoon salt (or less, to taste)
1/4 teaspoon garlic powder
2 to 3 tablespoons mayonnaise
1/2 pound fresh or imitation crabmeat or 1 (6-ounce) can crabmeat

PREHEAT OVEN TO 350°F. Cut English muffins in half. In a medium bowl, mix together butter, cheese, salt, garlic powder and mayonnaise. Stir in crabmeat. Spread on muffin halves. Leave whole for general eating, or cut into fourths for appetizers. (At this point, they may be frozen for later use.) Bake for 20 minutes, or until lightly browned and bubbly. They may also be popped in the microwave until bubbly, but they won't be crisp.

> **Carol's Corner**
>
> *Our friend Terri suggests that when a recipe calls for softened butter or cream cheese and you have forgotten to take it out of the refrigerator ahead of time, fill your mixing bowl with hot water, let it stand for a few minutes, then dump the water out and dry the bowl. The warmth from the bowl will help the butter or cream cheese to soften as you are mixing it with the other ingredients.*

Mountain Home Lodge

A n array of outdoor activities, first-class dining and friendly service make Mountain Home Lodge a serene resort for all seasons. Spring, summer and fall colors provide stunning backdrops for hiking, mountain biking, whitewater rafting, horseback riding, fishing, swimming and tennis.

Rated one of the region's most romantic getaways, the Lodge is also an ideal setting for small group seminars, weddings and family reunions.

INNKEEPERS:	*Brad & Kathy Schmidt*
ADDRESS:	*8201 Mountain Home Road*
	Leavenworth, WA 98826
TELEPHONE:	*(509) 548-7077; (800) 414-2378*
FAX:	*(509) 548-5008*
EMAIL:	*info@mthome.com*
WEBSITE:	*www.mthome.com*
ROOMS:	*9 Rooms; 1 Suite; 1 Cabin; All with private baths*
OPEN:	*Year-round*
CHILDREN:	*Specific guidelines for children (Call ahead)*
ANIMALS:	*Prohibited*
SMOKING:	*Prohibited*

Kathy's Basil Crostini

Makes 30-40 appetizers

Make one batch with regular pesto sauce and another batch with sun-dried tomato pesto sauce. Some crostini will be "green" and some will be "pink"—perfect for holiday entertaining. To "dress" them up, a small sliver of basil and/or sun-dried tomato can be added to the top of each crostini after broiling.

3/4 cup mayonnaise
1/4 cup Parmesan cheese, finely grated ("canned" type works better than freshly grated)
2 to 5 tablespoons prepared pesto sauce (regular or sun-dried tomato pesto sauce)
Baguette bread, thinly sliced

PREHEAT BROILER. In a small bowl, mix mayonnaise, cheese and pesto sauce together. (If you wish, more cheese or pesto can be added to suit taste.) Lightly toast baguette slices on one side under broiler. Generously spread mixture on the untoasted side of the slices and broil for about 3 minutes or until bubbly. Serve hot.

Optional cooking method: PREHEAT OVEN TO 400°F. Bake crostini for 10-15 minutes, or until light brown and crisp around edges.

Variation: Finely diced oil-packed sun-dried tomatoes (drained) can be added to regular pesto sauce.

Make-ahead tip: The pesto mixture can be made several days in advance and refrigerated.

Carol's Corner

We were delighted to have all three of our children, Kyle, Erin, and Ryan home for Christmas.
I fixed Kathy's Basil Crostini and they thought it was a winner! Try it for your next party or family gathering.

Chinaberry Hill

L ocated above the city streets of Tacoma, Chinaberry Hill is a grand Victorian estate surrounded by century-old trees, cascading greenery and captivating views of Puget Sound. This urban inn features an extensive collection of period furniture.

Downtown shops, Antique Row and the waterfront are all within a few blocks of this remarkable garden retreat.

INNKEEPERS:	*Cecil & Yarrow Wayman*
ADDRESS:	*302 Tacoma Avenue North*
	North Tacoma, WA 98403
TELEPHONE:	*(253) 272-1282*
FAX:	*(253) 272-1335*
EMAIL:	*chinaberry@wa.net*
WEBSITE:	*www.wa.net/chinaberry*
ROOMS:	*1 Room; 4 Suites; All with private baths*
OPEN:	*Year-round*
CHILDREN:	*Children are welcome in the guest cottage*
ANIMALS:	*Prohibited; Resident cats*
SMOKING:	*Permitted on verandah*

Jalapeño Swirls

Approximately 120 bite-size appetizers

Have fun, be adventurous! The filling combinations for this basic recipe are almost limitless—for a touch of the Pacific Northwest, try a combination of cream cheese, smoked salmon and diced green onions. Another sure-fire winner is diced red pepper, green onions and sliced black olives.

1 (7 or 8-ounce) can chopped green chiles, drained
1 tablespoon diced jalapeño peppers (or to taste, but watch out, they'll heat up after sitting in the cream cheese for awhile)
2 (8-ounce) packages of cream cheese, room temperature
1 (10-count) package extra large (burrito size) flour tortillas (the colored wraps are fun!)

In a medium bowl, mix together green chiles, jalapeños and cream cheese. Wrap tortillas in towel to keep moist and heat in oven, until pliable. Spread cream cheese mixture across tortillas, avoiding outer left and right edges, then roll up each tortilla tightly. Place rolled tortillas on a platter, cover with plastic wrap and chill for at least 30 minutes. Slice into 1/2-inch slices, discarding ends, and lay flat on an appetizer plate, so that the swirl pattern is face up.

Make-ahead tip: To make a day in advance, wrap each individual tortilla roll tightly in plastic wrap and refrigerate.

> *"Whenever we serve these, at least 1-2 people will come up and demand the recipe. When we share the process with them, it's always met with amazement - that something so simple can have such an elegant appeal. Fair warning: make plenty - people will eat a LOT of these - they're irresistible!"*
>
> Yarrow Wayman - Chinaberry Hill

Abendblume Pension

T he rooms at the Abendblume Pension Bed and Breakfast are spacious and comfortable. French doors open to a private balcony in the Rosengarten Room. Pine walls and a large river rock fireplace highlight the decor in the Tannenbaum Room.

Breakfast is tastefully prepared and served each morning in the traditional Austrian breakfast room.

INNKEEPERS:	*Randy & Renee Sexauer*
ADDRESS:	*12570 Ranger Road*
	Leavenworth, WA 98826
TELEPHONE:	*(509) 548-4059; (800) 669-7634*
FAX:	*(509) 548-9032*
EMAIL:	*abendblm@rightathome.com*
WEBSITE:	*www.abendblume.com*
ROOMS:	*7 Rooms; 4 Suites; All with private baths*
OPEN:	*Year-round*
CHILDREN:	*Prohibited*
ANIMALS:	*Prohibited*
SMOKING:	*Prohibited*

Salsa

Makes about 3 1/2 cups

Wash your hands thoroughly after removing the seeds and membranes from the jalapeño peppers (or wear rubber gloves). Otherwise, the juice and oils from the peppers can cause a burning sensation to your eyes if you accidentally touch them. If this should happen, flush your eyes immediately with water.

1 large garlic clove
2 to 6 jalapeño peppers, seeds and membranes removed
4 small tomatillos (about 1/2 cup), husks removed
6 plum tomatoes, diced (about 2 1/2 cups)
1 medium onion, finely diced (about 1/2 cup)
1/2 green bell pepper, finely diced (about 1/4 cup)
2 tablespoons coarsely chopped parsley
2 tablespoons coarsely chopped cilantro
Juice of 1 lime (about 2 tablespoons)
1/2 teaspoon salt (or more to taste)

In a food processor, finely chop garlic and jalapeño peppers. Add tomatillos and chop again. Place mixture into a large bowl and combine with remaining ingredients. The salsa can be served immediately, but it will be even better if flavors are allowed to blend by chilling several hours or overnight.

"For a salsa with more bite, add more jalapeños or some cumin. If you leave out the tomatillos, the salsa will be good, but it will taste more like a simple tomato salad."

Renee Sexauer - Abendblume Pension

Carol's Corner

A tomatillo is often called a Mexican green tomato. It is similar to a small green tomato in size, shape and appearance, but is covered with a thin parchment-like covering. Its flavor could best be described as a combination of apple, lemon and herbs. Tomatillos are available in most supermarkets or specialty produce stores. Remove the husks and wash the fruit before using.

Caswell's on the Bay

G uests of Caswell's on the Bay Bed and Breakfast relax in the spacious parlor with its breathtaking views of Willapa Bay, Long Island and the Coastal Mountains. This private getaway is a perfect setting for weddings, family reunions and group meetings.

Special features include freshly pressed 100% cotton sheets, safety locks on all guest rooms and the finest Caswell-Massey amenities.

INNKEEPERS:	*Bob & Marilyn Caswell*
ADDRESS:	*25204 Sandridge Road*
	Ocean Park, WA 98640
TELEPHONE:	*(360) 665-6535*
FAX:	*(360) 665-6500*
EMAIL:	*Not Available*
WEBSITE:	*www.site-works.com/caswells*
ROOMS:	*5 Rooms; All with private baths*
OPEN:	*Year-round*
CHILDREN:	*Children over the age of 12 are welcome*
ANIMALS:	*Prohibited*
SMOKING:	*Permitted outside only*

Microwave Caramel Corn

Makes 3 1/2 quarts

A treat sure to be enjoyed by everyone!

3 1/2 quarts (14 cups) popped popcorn
1/2 cup (1 stick) butter
1 cup brown sugar
1/4 cup light corn syrup
1/2 teaspoon salt
1/2 teaspoon baking powder

Lightly coat a piece of waxed paper (about 24-inches long) with nonstick cooking spray and set aside on counter or tabletop. Pop popcorn until you have the proper amount; discard any unpopped kernels. Place the popped popcorn in a large brown paper bag (grocery sack). In a medium-size heavy saucepan, melt butter. Add brown sugar, corn syrup and salt. (Make sure your pan is large enough, as this mixture bubbles up and "grows".) Bring to a boil over medium-high heat, stirring constantly. Boil for two minutes without stirring. Then give it a stir, and boil for two minutes more without stirring. Remove from heat. Add baking powder and stir thoroughly. Pour caramel mixture over popcorn and shake bag to mix. Put the bag of popcorn in the microwave on high for one minute. Shake bag to mix and put it back in the microwave for one minute more. Shake and pour popcorn out onto waxed paper. Use a spoon to scrape out any remaining caramel corn stuck to the bag. Let caramel corn cool completely. Store in an airtight container.

> **Carol's Corner**
>
> *Air-popped popcorn works great for this recipe. You can also use the low-fat microwave popcorn that comes in bags, but reduce the salt in the recipe to 1/4 teaspoon. The caramel corn can be frozen in freezer bags for later use, but if anyone knows it's in there, believe me, it won't last long!*

Desserts

Desserts

Ridgeway Farm

Nestled in the beautiful fields of the Skagit Valley, the Ridgeway Farm Bed and Breakfast is a 1928 Dutch Colonial farmhouse. Hiram Wells, the original homesteader, walked the "ridgeways" of the Skagit delta during flood periods.

Springtime in Skagit Valley is a grand celebration. Blooming tulips, daffodils and irises paint the valley in a rainbow of colors.

INNKEEPERS:	*Louise & John Kelly*
ADDRESS:	*14914 McLean Road*
	Mount Vernon, WA 98273
TELEPHONE:	*(360) 428-8068; (800) 428-8068*
FAX:	*(360) 428-8880*
EMAIL:	*ridgeway@halcyon.com*
WEBSITE:	*www.placestostay.com/lacon-ridgewayfarm*
ROOMS:	*7 Rooms; 1 Suite; 1 Cottage; Private & shared baths*
OPEN:	*Year-round*
CHILDREN:	*Children 12 and older are preferred*
ANIMALS:	*Prohibited*
SMOKING:	*Permitted outside only*

Apple Crumb Pie

Makes 6-8 servings

Great served hot or cold with a big scoop of vanilla ice cream!

5 to 7 medium apples, peeled, cored and sliced
1 (9-inch) unbaked pie shell
1/2 cup sugar
1 teaspoon cinnamon

Topping

3/4 cup flour
1/2 cup sugar
1/4 teaspoon cinnamon (or to taste, up to 1/2 teaspoon)
1/3 cup butter

PREHEAT OVEN TO 425°F. Place sliced apples in pie shell (it will be heaping). Mix sugar and cinnamon and sprinkle over apples. In a medium bowl, prepare topping by combining flour, sugar and cinnamon. Using a pastry blender, cut in butter until crumbly. Spoon topping over apples. Pat down gently. Bake in hot oven (425°F.) for 10 minutes. Reduce heat to 350°F. and bake an additional 35-45 minutes, or until apples are soft and topping is light brown.

The Manor Farm Inn

The welcome is warm at The Manor Farm Inn. From the gently winding, tree-lined country road to the stately white house with its manicured lawns, this private oasis offers tranquillity and seclusion from the bustle of Puget Sound's cities.

Guests awaken to the aroma of hot-from-the-oven scones, served with homemade raspberry jam. Later, a three-course gourmet breakfast is served in the dining room.

INNKEEPERS:	*Jill & Don Day*
ADDRESS:	*26069 Big Valley Road NE*
	Poulsbo, WA 98370
TELEPHONE:	*(360) 779-4628*
FAX:	*(360) 779-4876*
EMAIL:	*office@manorfarminn.com*
WEBSITE:	*www.manorfarminn.com*
ROOMS:	*7 Rooms; All with private baths*
OPEN:	*Year-round*
CHILDREN:	*Children over the age of 16 are welcome*
ANIMALS:	*Prohibited*
SMOKING:	*Permitted outside only*

Manor Farm Inn
Blackberry-Apple Crumble

Makes 16 servings or feeds a horse

Served warm with ice cream, a real winner!

6 Granny Smith apples, peeled, cored and sliced
2 pounds fresh blackberries or 2 (1-pound) bags frozen blackberries
1 cup sugar
2 teaspoons cinnamon

Topping

3 cups flour
3 cups brown sugar
1 1/2 cups rolled oats
1 1/2 cups (3 sticks) butter, melted

PREHEAT OVEN TO 350°F. Coat a 14x12-inch deep-dish pan (or two 13x9-inch baking dishes can be used) with nonstick cooking spray. Place apples in bottom of dish. Then layer with blackberries. In a small bowl, mix together sugar and cinnamon and sprinkle over blackberries/apples. In a large bowl, mix together all topping ingredients. Crumble over blackberries and apples. Bake for 60 minutes, or until top is golden brown.

Note: For a smaller group, this recipe can be cut in half and baked in a 13x9-inch baking dish.

Carol's Corner

This luscious dessert showcases two of Washington's most delectable fruits—apples and blackberries. The combination of flavors is most pleasing. This recipe doesn't take long to put together, and yet it feeds a crowd.

Harborside

L ocated at the end of a winding driveway, surrounded by green ferns and a peaceful pond, the Harborside Bed and Breakfast is tranquillity at its best. Guests enjoy a private entrance, complete kitchen, patio and a deep moorage area and dock.

"On the water privacy."

~ Owners, Harborside B & B

INNKEEPERS:	*Terry & Joyce Galligan*
ADDRESS:	*8708 Goodman Dr. N.W.*
	Gig Harbor, WA 98332
TELEPHONE:	*(253) 851-1795*
FAX:	*(253) 858-2895*
EMAIL:	*Not Available*
WEBSITE:	*Not Available*
ROOMS:	*1 Suite; Private bath*
OPEN:	*Year-round*
CHILDREN:	*Welcome*
ANIMALS:	*Small dogs welcome (Prior approval for large pets)*
SMOKING:	*Permitted outside only*

Blackberry Cobbler

Makes 6 servings

This is an old-fashioned comfort food! Serve warm with whipping cream or ice cream.

1/2 cup sugar (or to taste, up to 3/4 cup)
1 tablespoon cornstarch
4 cups blackberries
1 teaspoon lemon juice

Biscuit Topping

1 cup flour
1 tablespoon + 1 teaspoon sugar, divided
1 1/2 teaspoon baking powder
1/2 teaspoon salt
3 tablespoons shortening
1/2 cup + 1 tablespoon milk, divided

PREHEAT OVEN TO 400°F. In a medium saucepan, stir together sugar and cornstarch. Add berries and lemon juice. Cook, stirring constantly, until mixture thickens and boils. Boil and stir 1 minute. Pour into ungreased 2-quart baking dish. Place in oven while preparing biscuit topping. In a small bowl, stir together flour, 1 tablespoon sugar, baking powder and salt. Add shortening and 1/2 cup milk. Cut through with 2 knives or pastry blender 6 times. Using a spoon, mix until dough forms a ball. Remove hot berries from oven. Drop dough by 6 spoonfuls onto berries. Brush tops of biscuits with remaining tablespoon of milk and sprinkle with remaining teaspoon of sugar. Return dish to oven (use potholders, dish is still very hot!) and bake, uncovered, for 25-30 minutes, or until biscuit topping is golden brown and berry mixture is bubbly.

Willcox House

O riginally built in 1937 by Colonel Julian and Constance Willcox, the Willcox House Country Inn has been restored to its art deco grandeur. Once described as the grand entertainment capital of the canal region, this elegant getaway continues that tradition.

Dinner is available to inn guests and a limited number of visitors. The elaborate four-course chef's choice meals attract diners from around the peninsula.

INNKEEPERS:	*Phillip & Cecilia Hughes*
ADDRESS:	*2390 Tekiu Road N.W.*
	Seabeck, WA 98380
TELEPHONE:	*(360) 830-4492; (800) 725-9477*
FAX:	*(360) 830-0506*
EMAIL:	*Not Available*
WEBSITE:	*www.willcoxhouse.com*
ROOMS:	*5 Rooms; All with private baths*
OPEN:	*Year-round*
CHILDREN:	*Children over 15 welcome (Younger children, individual basis)*
ANIMALS:	*Prohibited*
SMOKING:	*Prohibited*

Lemon Pudding Cake

Makes 4 servings

This refreshing dessert forms two layers as it bakes.

3 eggs, separated
1 cup sugar, divided
4 tablespoons butter, melted
1/3 cup flour
1/3 cup lemon juice
Zest of 1 lemon (grated peel)
1 cup milk, warmed
Red raspberries (or berries of choice)
Whipped cream (optional)
Mint leaves (optional)

PREHEAT OVEN TO 350°F. Separate eggs, putting egg whites in a small bowl and egg yolks in a large bowl. Beat egg yolks with about 1/2 of the sugar and melted butter. Alternately add flour and lemon juice. Mix in grated lemon peel. Set aside. Beat egg whites until foamy. Add rest of the sugar and beat until glossy and stiff. Set aside. Add the warmed milk to the egg yolk mixture. Then fold egg whites into the egg yolk mixture. Lightly butter or grease a 2-3 quart round bowl and pour in mixture. Set bowl into pan of hot water and bake for 45 minutes, or until top is lightly browned. Spoon into individual serving dishes and garnish with red raspberries, a touch of whipped cream and a fresh mint leaf.

Bosch Gärten

T he Bosch Gärten Bed and Breakfast was built in 1992 specifically as a bed and breakfast facility. Guests gaze out the floor-to-ceiling windows at the arbored rose garden and magnificent Cascade Mountains that tower in the southwest.

The Bavarian Village, with its many unique shops and excellent restaurants, is within easy walking distance.

INNKEEPERS:	*Cal & Myke Bosch*
ADDRESS:	*9846 Dye Road*
	Leavenworth, WA 98826
TELEPHONE:	*(509) 548-6900; (800) 535-0069*
FAX:	*(509) 548-6076*
EMAIL:	*Not Available*
WEBSITE:	*www.boschgärten.com*
ROOMS:	*3 Rooms; All with private baths*
OPEN:	*Year-round*
CHILDREN:	*School age children are welcome*
ANIMALS:	*Prohibited*
SMOKING:	*Prohibited*

Chocolate Mousse

Makes 8 servings

This dessert, perfect for chocoholics, is easy to make, but plan ahead as all ingredients, as well as bowl and beaters, must be thoroughly chilled.

2/3 cup chocolate syrup
2/3 of a (14-ounce) can sweetened condensed milk
2 cups heavy whipping cream
1/2 teaspoon vanilla
1/2 cup slivered almonds, for garnish (optional)
Whipped cream, for garnish (optional)
Chocolate shavings, for garnish (optional)

In a large bowl, mix together chocolate syrup, sweetened condensed milk, whipping cream and vanilla. Place in refrigerator, along with beaters, to chill. When well chilled, beat mixture until thick and stands in peaks. Spoon mixture into pretty demitasse cups. Freeze. Remove from freezer 15-20 minutes before serving. Garnish with a sprinkling of almonds or a dollop of whipped cream and chocolate shavings.

"This is not low in cholesterol or calories! Very rich! Yumm!"

Myke Bosch - Bosch Gärten

Island Escape

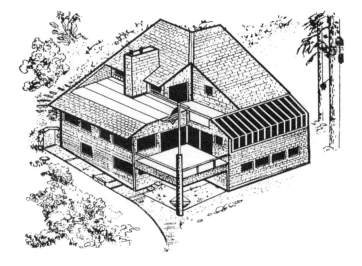

Nestled on the bluffs of Puget Sound, Island Escape Bed and Breakfast features a one-room suite that includes a separate living room with gas fireplace. This romantic getaway is beautifully landscaped with an array of seasonal flowers.

Guests select a savory breakfast from an assortment of gourmet meals that is served outside their door at a time they choose.

INNKEEPERS:	*Paula E. Pascoe*
ADDRESS:	*210 Island Boulevard*
	Fox Island, WA 98333
TELEPHONE:	*(253) 549-2044*
FAX:	*Not Available*
EMAIL:	*islandescape@narrows.com*
WEBSITE:	*www.narrows.com/islandescape*
ROOMS:	*1 Suite; Private bath*
OPEN:	*Year-round*
CHILDREN:	*Welcome*
ANIMALS:	*Prohibited*
SMOKING:	*Prohibited*

Paula's Easy Decadent Chocolate Trifle

Makes 10-12 servings

A clear glass trifle bowl will reveal every luscious layer!

1 chocolate cake mix (with pudding in the mix) <u>or</u> your favorite chocolate cake recipe
3 eggs (number <u>could</u> vary depending on which mix or recipe you use; follow directions on box)
1/3 to 1/2 cup oil (amount depends on which mix or recipe you use)
1 (16-ounce) can Hershey's chocolate syrup
6 (1.4-ounce) Hershey's SKOR bars, crushed
2 (12-ounce) tubs of Cool Whip, thawed in refrigerator
3 maraschino cherries with stems, drained, for garnish

Grease a 13x9-inch pan. Sprinkle flour or plain breadcrumbs on bottom and sides of pan. Mix and bake cake per box instructions. Once cooled, break cake into bite-size pieces and layer 1/3 of cake into a large glass bowl. Pour 1/3 of the chocolate syrup over cake pieces. Sprinkle approximately 1/3 of the crushed SKOR bars over syrup. (Set aside a spoonful of crushed bars to use for garnish later.) Spoon a layer of Cool Whip over all. Repeat all layers two more times, ending with Cool Whip. Sprinkle reserved SKOR pieces on top of the dessert. Add cherries to complete the decorating. Chill for <u>several</u> hours or overnight.

"This dessert presents beautifully in a glass bowl and you will have people asking for seconds!"

Paula Pascoe - Island Escape

Carol's Corner

This can also be made in individual pieces of clear stemware. Place the stemware on doily covered plates. Top each dessert with a bright red maraschino cherry. Very eye-appealing!

Willcox House

Providing warm hospitality since 1989, the Willcox House is a premier country house inn located between Seattle and the Olympic Peninsula on the Kitsap Peninsula. Surrounded by a natural paradise, every room has a commanding view of the Hood Canal and the Olympic Mountains. The private pier can accommodate boats or float planes.

Activities include beach-combing on the oyster-laden beach, swimming and boating.

INNKEEPERS:	*Phillip & Cecilia Hughes*
ADDRESS:	*2390 Tekiu Road N.W.*
	Seabeck, WA 98380
TELEPHONE:	*(360) 830-4492; (800) 725-9477*
FAX:	*(360) 830-0506*
EMAIL:	*Not Available*
WEBSITE:	*www.willcoxhouse.com*
ROOMS:	*5 Rooms; All with private baths*
OPEN:	*Year-round*
CHILDREN:	*Children over 15 are welcome (Younger children, individual basis)*
ANIMALS:	*Prohibited*
SMOKING:	*Prohibited*

Chocolate Truffle Cake

Serves 10-12

8 ounces semi-sweet baking chocolate
3/4 cup (1 1/2 sticks) butter
8 egg whites
6 egg yolks
1 teaspoon vanilla
1/4 cup strong brewed coffee, cooled to room temperature
2 tablespoons cognac <u>or</u> orange liqueur
1/3 cup flour
1/4 teaspoon cream of tartar
3/4 cup sugar

PREHEAT OVEN TO 350°F. In a small bowl, melt chocolate and butter together in microwave on low power, stirring frequently. (This step can also be done in a small saucepan over low heat.) Set aside. Separate eggs, putting the 8 egg whites in a large bowl and putting the 6 egg yolks in another large bowl. (Discard two egg yolks or save to use in another recipe.) Beat egg yolks with vanilla until light in color, about 5 minutes. Mix in the coffee. Add the cognac alternately with the flour. Mix the chocolate/butter mixture in with the egg yolk mixture and set aside. Beat the egg whites with cream of tartar until foamy. Add the sugar and beat until egg whites are glossy and form soft peaks. Using a wire whisk, fold a big scoop of egg whites into the chocolate mixture. Then fold in rest of the egg whites. Oil a 9-inch springform pan. Pour in batter and bake for 60 minutes. Cool <u>completely</u> on wire rack. (Cake will fall a bit in the middle when cooling.) Run knife around edge of pan and remove outer rim. Cover and refrigerate cake. When ready to serve, bring to room temperature. Serve individual slices with fresh berries, berry coulis (purée or sauce), caramel or vanilla sauce.

<u>Make-ahead tip</u>: Freeze cake on cookie sheet for an hour or so. Then wrap well and freeze for later use. Thaw in refrigerator.

Mimi's Cottage by the Sea

L ocated on Vashon Island, Mimi's Cottage by the Sea is a quiet country getaway that is only a 15-minute ferry ride from Seattle or Tacoma. Surrounded by a hillside garden and just a short walk from the beach, this island escape reflects a rural, relaxed lifestyle.

"We don't know whether to tell our friends or keep it a secret for ourselves."

~ Guest, Mimi's Cottage

INNKEEPERS:	*Gloria Olson*
ADDRESS:	*7923 S.W. Hawthorne Lane*
	Vashon Island, WA 98070
TELEPHONE:	*(206) 567-4383*
FAX:	*(206) 567-4383 (Call ahead)*
EMAIL:	*Not Available*
WEBSITE:	*Not Available*
ROOMS:	*2 Rooms; 1 Cottage; All with private baths*
OPEN:	*Year-round*
CHILDREN:	*Prohibited*
ANIMALS:	*Prohibited*
SMOKING:	*Prohibited*

Mimi's Orange-Coconut Truffles

Makes approximately 48 truffles

Since these truffles are great to eat frozen, keep some in your freezer for unexpected drop-in guests.

1/2 cup (1 stick) butter, room temperature
1 (1-pound) box powdered sugar
1 (6-ounce) can frozen orange juice concentrate, thawed
1 (12-ounce) box vanilla wafers, crushed (use about 70 wafers, you will have a few left over to eat!)
1 cup toasted chopped pecans (directions below)
1 (12-ounce) package shredded or flaked coconut

In a large bowl, combine butter, powdered sugar, orange juice concentrate and crushed vanilla wafers. (The number of vanilla wafers is approximate. You can use a few less or a few more and still get great results.) Add cooled pecans and mix well. (Mixture will be stiff). Balls can be formed right away or mixture can be covered and chilled in refrigerator for several hours or overnight. Roll into 3/4-inch balls, then roll balls in coconut. Refrigerate or freeze. They may be served chilled or frozen.

To toast pecans: Place nuts on a cookie sheet in a 350°F. oven for about 8-10 minutes.

Carol's Corner

When my brother Gordon and sister-in-law Lynn were visiting, we took a trip to Victoria, BC. We brought along Mimi's Orange-Coconut Truffles, Frosted Zucchini Bars and Jenny's Norwegian Brown Bread. All three recipes got a "thumb's up" as we savored them on the ferry with steaming hot Starbucks coffee.

MacKaye Harbor Inn

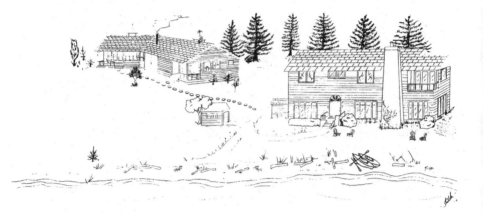

Tranquillity, romance and a touch of nostalgia await the guests of the MacKaye Harbor Inn. Originally built in 1904 and completely restored in 1985, this charming inn offers five beautifully decorated guest rooms, each reminiscent of the past.

The carriage house, built in 1991, has added two large luxury accommodations in the same MacKaye Harbor Inn tradition.

INNKEEPERS:	*Robin & Mike Bergstrom*
ADDRESS:	*Route 1; PO Box 1940*
	Lopez Island, WA 98261
TELEPHONE:	*(360) 468-2253*
FAX:	*(360) 468-2393*
EMAIL:	*mckay@pacificrim.net*
WEBSITE:	*www.pacificrim.net/~mckay*
ROOMS:	*4 Rooms; 1 Suite; 2 Cottages; Private and shared baths*
OPEN:	*Year-round*
CHILDREN:	*Children nine and older are welcome*
ANIMALS:	*Prohibited*
SMOKING:	*Prohibited*

Cowboy Cookies

Makes 3 1/2 to 4 dozen (3-inch) cookies

Try dropping the dough onto the cookie sheet with a small ice cream scoop (1 3/4-inch in diameter). It's easy and makes uniform-size cookies.

1 cup sugar
1 cup brown sugar
1 cup shortening
3 eggs
1 teaspoon vanilla
2 cups flour
1/2 teaspoon baking powder
1 teaspoon baking soda
1/2 teaspoon salt
2 cups rolled oats
2 cups chocolate chips

PREHEAT OVEN TO 350°F. In a large bowl, beat together sugar, brown sugar and shortening. Mix in eggs and vanilla. Sift in flour, baking powder, baking soda and salt. Add oats and mix well. Stir in chocolate chips. Drop dough onto greased cookie sheet and bake for approximately 15 minutes. Let rest on cookie sheet a couple minutes and then transfer cookies to a wire rack to cool.

"I can make these with my eyes shut! This cookie has become the standby for the inn, as most people never turn down a chocolate chip cookie, especially one with healthy oatmeal in it and fresh out of the oven."

Robin Bergstrom - MacKaye Harbor Inn

Spring Bay Inn

Early risers of the Spring Bay Inn on Orcas Island are treated to a complimentary breakfast that includes homemade pastries, fresh fruits, coffees and teas. Brunch, also included, is served family-style in the bay-front dining room.

Weather permitting, a daily kayak tour provides guests a unique way to explore the natural beauty of the island's waterfront.

INNKEEPERS:	*Carl Burger & Sandy Playa*
ADDRESS:	*Obstruction Pass Trailhead Road*
	Olga, Orcas Island WA 98279
TELEPHONE:	*(360) 376-5531*
FAX:	*(360) 376-2193*
EMAIL:	*kayakinn@rockisland.com*
WEBSITE:	*www.springbayinn.com*
ROOMS:	*5 Rooms; All with private baths*
OPEN:	*Year-round*
CHILDREN:	*Children are welcome (Must be over 10 to kayak)*
ANIMALS:	*Prohibited*
SMOKING:	*Prohibited*

Oatmeal Raisin Cookies

Makes approximately 3 dozen (3-inch) cookies

For variety, next time try dried cranberries in place of the raisins.

1 cup butter, melted
2 cups brown sugar
2 eggs
2 teaspoons vanilla
1 1/2 cups flour
1 teaspoon salt
1 teaspoon baking soda
1 teaspoon cinnamon
3 cups rolled oats
1 cup walnuts
1 cup raisins

PREHEAT OVEN TO 375°F. In a large bowl, mix together melted butter, brown sugar, eggs and vanilla. Sift in flour, salt, soda and cinnamon; mix well. Stir in oats, nuts and raisins. Drop dough by spoonfuls onto a greased cookie sheet and bake for about 10 minutes. Note: Take out of oven before they look fully cooked; they will firm up when they cool. Leave on cookie sheet several minutes to cool before removing to wire rack.

Duffy House

The Duffy House Bed and Breakfast is a 1920's Tudor-style home that is conveniently located on a scenic jogging and bicycling loop that begins and ends at the ferry terminal. A full breakfast, featuring freshly baked goods, complements the lodging experience.

Local activities include golfing, sportfishing, sailing, whale watching from strategic settings, exploring tidal pools, following the flight of a bald eagle or biking the byways.

INNKEEPERS:	*Mary & Arthur Miller*
ADDRESS:	*760 Pear Point Road*
	Friday Harbor, WA 98250
TELEPHONE:	*(360) 378-5604; (800) 972-2089*
FAX:	*(360) 378-6535*
EMAIL:	*duffyhouse@rockisland.com*
WEBSITE:	*www.pacificrim.net/~bydesign/duffy.html*
ROOMS:	*5 Rooms; All with private baths*
OPEN:	*Year-round*
CHILDREN:	*Children eight and older are welcome*
ANIMALS:	*Prohibited*
SMOKING:	*Permitted outside only*

Snickerdoodles

Makes about 4 dozen (3 1/2-inch) cookies

Bet you can't eat just one! These cookies are crisp around the edges, yet remain soft and chewy in the middle. Perfect!

1 cup (2 sticks) butter, room temperature
2 cups sugar
2 eggs
3 cups flour
2 teaspoons cream of tartar
1 teaspoon baking soda

Topping

1/4 cup sugar
2 teaspoons cinnamon

PREHEAT OVEN TO 400°F. In a large bowl, beat together butter and sugar. Add eggs, one at a time, beating well after each addition. Sift in flour, cream of tartar and baking soda. Mix well. Chill. Drop dough 2-inches apart (they spread while baking) on ungreased cookie sheet and press flat (use fingertips or heel of hand). Combine topping ingredients to make sugar/cinnamon mixture. Sprinkle on top of the cookies. Bake for 6-7 minutes. (They will be pale and not look done.) Let rest on the cookie sheet a minute or two and remove to wire rack to cool.

Carol's Corner

Ten-year-old neighbor Charlee dropped by one day while I was testing this recipe. Valuing her opinion, I gave her some Snickerdoodles and asked her to let me know what she thought. After she and her family tasted them, she reported, "This recipe should be in the book!" So, Charlee, here it is. This one's especially for you!

Mill Town Manor

E ach of the spacious rooms at the Mill Town Manor Bed and Breakfast has its own distinct personality and are filled with antiques and 1920's memorabilia. The Garbo Room recreates a dressing room of this famous elusive actress. The Babe Room, named after Babe Ruth, celebrates the early glory days of baseball.

The Valentino Room features hemlock flooring and private his and her dressing rooms.

INNKEEPERS:	*Gary & Debbi Saint*
ADDRESS:	*116 Oak Street*
	Eatonville, WA 98328
TELEPHONE:	*(360) 832-6506*
FAX:	*(360) 832-6506*
EMAIL:	*milltown@foxinternet.net*
WEBSITE:	*www.bbonline.com/wa/milltown/*
ROOMS:	*5 Rooms; All with private baths*
OPEN:	*Year-round*
CHILDREN:	*Children six and older are welcome*
ANIMALS:	*Prohibited*
SMOKING:	*Prohibited*

Chewy Molasses Crinkles

Makes about 3 dozen cookies

3/4 cup shortening or margarine, room temperature
1 cup + 1/4 cup sugar, divided
1/4 cup molasses
1 egg
2 cups flour
2 teaspoons baking soda
1 teaspoon cinnamon
1/2 teaspoon ground cloves
1/2 teaspoon ground ginger
1/2 teaspoon salt

In a large bowl, beat together shortening, 1 cup sugar (reserve the 1/4 cup for later use), molasses and egg. Sift in flour, baking soda, cinnamon, cloves, ginger and salt. Mix well and chill for at least 30 minutes. PREHEAT OVEN TO 375°F. Form dough into 1-inch balls and roll in reserved sugar. Place balls on greased cookie sheet. Press fingertip in center of each, making a slight indentation. Bake for 8-10 minutes for a chewy cookie, or 10-12 minutes for a crisp cookie.

MacKaye Harbor Inn

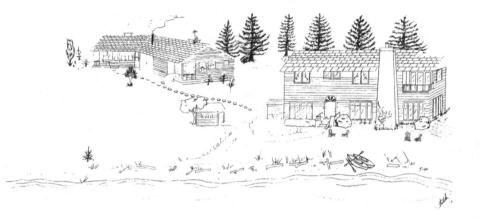

T he MacKaye Harbor Inn is a quiet retreat for those seeking comfort, beauty and peace. Located on Lopez Island, this private getaway has been a beacon showing safe harbor to sailors, fishermen and travelers since the turn-of-the-century.

Special comforts include a water view from the spacious parlor, down comforters, a beverage bar, guest refrigerator and a bountiful breakfast.

INNKEEPERS:	*Robin & Mike Bergstrom*
ADDRESS:	*Route 1; PO Box 1940*
	Lopez Island, WA 98261
TELEPHONE:	*(360) 468-2253*
FAX:	*(360) 468-2393*
EMAIL:	*mckay@pacificrim.net*
WEBSITE:	*www.pacificrim.net/~mckay*
ROOMS:	*4 Rooms; 1 Suite; 2 Cottages; Private and*
	shared baths
OPEN:	*Year-round*
CHILDREN:	*Children nine and older are welcome*
ANIMALS:	*Prohibited*
SMOKING:	*Prohibited*

Coconut Shortbread

Makes about 2 dozen wedge-shaped cookies

Buttery and rich! Perfect with afternoon tea!

4 cups sweetened coconut
2 cups flour
9 tablespoons sugar
1 teaspoon salt
1 cup (2 sticks) unsalted butter, room temperature
1 1/2 teaspoons vanilla

Lightly butter two 9-inch diameter tart pans with removable bottoms. In a large bowl, mix coconut, flour, sugar and salt. Add butter and vanilla and beat well with an electric mixer. Divide dough between pans and press to cover bottoms. Refrigerate 15 minutes. PREHEAT OVEN TO 350°F. Bake for 30-40 minutes. Remove pan sides and cut shortbread into wedges. If wedges are moist, place on cookie sheet and bake until crisp, about 7 more minutes. Store shortbread in an airtight container at room temperature.

The Inn at Burg's Landing

F rom the large picture window of The Inn at Burg's Landing, guests view sailboats gliding past the island and ocean freighters and barges en route to Tacoma or Olympia.

Two miles from the inn sits a one-room schoolhouse that innkeeper Ken Burg attended as a child. One mile from the schoolhouse is the Johnson Farm, now the Anderson Island Historical Society Museum.

INNKEEPERS:	*Ken & Annie Burg*
ADDRESS:	*8808 Villa Beach Road*
	Anderson Island, WA 98303
TELEPHONE:	*(253) 884-9185; (800) 431-5622*
FAX:	*Not Available*
EMAIL:	*innatburgslanding@mailexcite.com*
WEBSITE:	*Not Available*
ROOMS:	*4 Rooms; Private and shared baths*
OPEN:	*Year-round*
CHILDREN:	*Children are welcome*
ANIMALS:	*Prohibited*
SMOKING:	*Permitted on outside deck*

Biscotti

Makes about 3 1/2 dozen cookies

Vary the taste of these twice-baked crunchy Italian cookies by using different extract flavorings. Great for dipping in coffee!

4 cups flour
1 cup sugar
1 1/2 teaspoons baking powder
1/4 teaspoon salt
4 eggs
1 cup oil
3 teaspoons vanilla (or almond, orange or anise flavorings)
1/4 cup coarsely chopped almonds
Semi-sweet chocolate (optional)
Crushed almonds (optional)

PREHEAT OVEN TO 375°F. In a large bowl, sift together flour, sugar, baking powder and salt. In a small bowl, lightly beat together eggs, oil and vanilla. Add egg mixture and chopped almonds to dry ingredients. Stir until combined. Divide dough into 4 equal pieces. Form into loaves, each about 3-inches wide and 1 1/2-inches high. Place 3 or 4-inches apart on ungreased cookie sheet. Bake for 20-25 minutes. Remove from oven and let cool for 10 minutes. Transfer loaves to cutting board. With serrated knife, cut each loaf crosswise into 1/2-inch thick diagonal slices. Place slices cut-side down on cookie sheet in a single layer and bake for an additional 10-15 minutes, or until golden brown, turning once. Transfer to wire racks; cool completely. Store in an airtight container.

For chocolate-dipped biscotti: Melt semi-sweet chocolate in a microwave oven or over low heat on the stovetop. Dip tops, sides or bottoms of biscotti into chocolate. If desired, sprinkle some crushed almonds over chocolate. Refrigerate biscotti about 30 minutes to set chocolate. Store in a tightly covered container.

Alphabetical Listing of Bed & Breakfasts

(Continued on next page)

Alphabetical Listing of Bed & Breakfasts

Alphabetical Listing of Bed & Breakfasts

Weights and Measures Equivalents

By making a few conversions, cooks not accustomed to the U.S. measurement system can still make the recipes found in the *Washington State Bed & Breakfast Cookbook*. Use the helpful charts below and on the opposite page to find the metric equivalents.

OVEN TEMPERATURE EQUIVALENTS		
FAHRENHEIT	**CELSIUS**	**GAS SETTING**
250	120	1/2
275	140	1
300	150	2
325	160	3
350	180	4
375	190	5
400	200	6
425	220	7
450	230	8
475	240	9
500	260	10

BAKING PAN SIZES	
AMERICAN	**METRIC**
11x7x1 1/2-inch baking pan	28x18x4-centimeter baking pan
13x9x2-inch baking pan	32.5x23x5-centimeter baking pan
15x10x2-inch baking pan	38x25.5x2.5-centimeter baking pan (Swiss roll tin)
9-inch pie plate	22x4- or 23x4-inch centimeter pie plate
9x5x3-inch loaf pan	23x13x6-centimeter or 2-pound narrow loaf pan
1 1/2-quart casserole	1.5-liter casserole

Weights and Measures Equivalents

LENGTH MEASURES	
1/8 inch	3 millimeters
1/4 inch	6 millimeters
1/2 inch	12 millimeters
1 inch	2.5 centimeters

LIQUID AND DRY MEASURES	
U.S.	**METRIC** **(VALUES HAVE BEEN ROUNDED)**
1/4 teaspoon	1.25 milliliters
1/2 teaspoon	2.5 milliliters
1 teaspoon	5 milliliters
1 tablespoon (3 teaspoons)	15 milliliters
1 fluid ounce (2 tablespoons)	30 milliliters
1/4 cup	60 milliliters
1/3 cup	80 milliliters
1 cup	240 milliliters
1 pint (2 cups)	480 milliliters
1 quart (4 cups, 32 ounces)	960 milliliters
1 gallon (4 quarts)	3.84 liters
1 ounce (by weight)	28 grams
1/4 pound (4 ounces)	114 grams
1 pound	454 grams
2 1/4 pounds	1 kilogram

High-Altitude Adjustment Suggestions

If you live in a high-altitude region, you may find it necessary to make some minor adjustments when baking. This is due to the following facts:

- Air pressure is lower at any altitude above sea level. This lower pressure causes baked foods to rise faster.
- The atmosphere at higher altitudes is drier; consequently, flour is drier and will absorb more liquid.
- Foods take longer to cook at high altitudes.
- Liquids evaporate more rapidly at higher altitudes.

Although there are no hard and fast rules, the following guide will help you make adjustments in your favorite cake recipes. Since every recipe is different, you may have to experiment a few times with each recipe to discover the best proportions. Start by making the first two suggested changes. If this doesn't seem to be enough, next time try another one or two of the suggested adjustments. With experimentation, you will become successful!

CAKE RECIPE ADJUSTMENT GUIDE FOR HIGH ALTITUDES			
ADJUSTMENT	**3,000 FT.**	**5,000 FT.**	**7,000 FT.**
Baking powder: For each teaspoon, decrease	1/8 teaspoon	1/8 to 1/4 teaspoon	1/4 teaspoon
Sugar: For each cup, decrease	1 to 2 tablespoons	2 to 4 tablespoons	3 to 4 tablespoons
Fat: For each cup, decrease	1 to 2 tablespoons	2 to 4 tablespoons	3 to 4 tablespoons
Liquid: For each cup, add	1 to 2 tablespoons	2 to 4 tablespoons	3 to 4 tablespoons
Temperature: Increase	15° F.	15 to 25° F.	20 to 25° F.

HELPFUL HINTS FOR OTHER HIGH-ALTITUDE COOKING

Cookies: For cake-type cookies, reduce sugar by 3 tablespoons per cup. For drop cookies, test bake 2 or 3 cookies. If they flatten too much, add 2 to 4 tablespoons flour.

Pie Crusts: May require slightly more liquid but are baked at the same temperature.

Yeast Breads: May require a shorter rising time and should rise only until double in bulk. Use slightly less flour, judging by the feel of the dough.

 All recipes in the *Washington State Bed & Breakfast Cookbook* were tested at sea level.

Index

Index

Index

Index

Index

Index

Index

Index

About the Authors

Carol McCollum Faino, an Iowa native and former teacher, has been intrigued with the bed and breakfast concept for years. She and her husband Rod have enjoyed staying in numerous B & B's and country inns during their many travels and frequent moves around the United States. Carol's passion for writing bed and breakfast cookbooks is a natural culmination of combining this favorite pastime with her longtime interest in cooking. Carol and her husband live in a 93-year-old historic home in the Puget Sound Naval Shipyard in Bremerton, Washington. They have three grown children, Kyle, Erin and Ryan.

Doreen Kaitfors Hazledine grew up on a ranch in western South Dakota. She has worked as a teacher, administrator, businesswoman and screenwriter. One of her screenplays is presently in development. Doreen, a former Mrs. South Dakota, lives with her husband, Don, in Denver, Colorado.

Order Form for Peppermint Press B & B Cookbooks

Please ask in your local bookstore for the *Washington State Bed & Breakfast Cookbook* or the *Colorado Bed & Breakfast Cookbook*. Or you may order directly from Peppermint Press. Books will be shipped immediately. We accept VISA, MASTERCARD and CHECKS.

Please send me _____ copies of the
WASHINGTON STATE BED & BREAKFAST COOKBOOK @ $21.95 each _____
   (Colorado residents add $1.60 tax per book) _____
   Shipping and handling: Add $3.00 per book _____
   (Canadian and overseas orders add $10.00 per book for shipping)

Please send me _____ copies of the
COLORADO BED & BREAKFAST COOKBOOK @ $18.95 each _____
   (Colorado residents add $1.38 tax per book) _____
   Shipping and handling: Add $3.00 per book _____
   (Canadian and overseas orders add $10.00 per book for shipping)

SAVE! Please send me _____ VALUE PACKS* @ $35.00 each _____
*Each VALUE PACK contains 1 Colorado book and 1 Washington book
   (Colorado residents add $2.56 tax per Value Pack) _____
   Shipping and handling: Add $5.00 per Value Pack _____
   (Canadian and overseas orders add $15.00 per Value Pack for shipping)

                                     TOTAL: _____

Please make checks payable to: **Peppermint Press**
(Payable in U.S. dollars only. No C.O.D.'s or Cash.)

Name _____ Street _____

City _____ State ____ Zip _____ Tel _____

Please charge to my VISA ____ or MasterCard ____

Card number _____ Exp _____

Cardholder's signature _____

Send order form to:

Peppermint Press • PO Box 370235 • Denver, CO 80237-0235
or
TEL: (800) 758-0803   FAX: (303) 369-7907
EMAIL: bbcookbook@aol.com • WEBSITE: www.bbcookbook.com

Great Adventures!   Great Food!

Colorado Bed & Breakfast Cookbook

Washington State Bed & Breakfast Cookbook

Get your copies today!

Order Form for Peppermint Press B & B Cookbooks

Please ask in your local bookstore for the *Washington State Bed & Breakfast Cookbook* or the *Colorado Bed & Breakfast Cookbook*. Or you may order directly from Peppermint Press. Books will be shipped immediately. We accept VISA, MASTERCARD and CHECKS.

Please send me_____copies of the
WASHINGTON STATE BED & BREAKFAST COOKBOOK @ $21.95 each _____
 (Colorado residents add $1.60 tax per book)   _____
 Shipping and handling: Add $3.00 per book   _____
 (Canadian and overseas orders add $10.00 per book for shipping)

Please send me_____copies of the
COLORADO BED & BREAKFAST COOKBOOK @ $18.95 each   _____
 (Colorado residents add $1.38 tax per book)   _____
 Shipping and handling: Add $3.00 per book   _____
 (Canadian and overseas orders add $10.00 per book for shipping)

SAVE! Please send me _____VALUE PACKS* @ $35.00 each   _____
*Each VALUE PACK contains 1 Colorado book and 1 Washington book
 (Colorado residents add $2.56 tax per Value Pack)   _____
 Shipping and handling: Add $5.00 per Value Pack   _____
 (Canadian and overseas orders add $15.00 per Value Pack for shipping)

             TOTAL: _____

Please make checks payable to: **Peppermint Press**
(Payable in U.S. dollars only. No C.O.D.'s or Cash.)

Name_____ Street _____

City_____ State____ Zip _____ Tel _____

Please charge to my VISA ____ or MasterCard ____

Card number _____ Exp_____

Cardholder's signature _____

Send order form to:

Peppermint Press • PO Box 370235 • Denver, CO 80237-0235

or

TEL: (800) 758-0803 FAX: (303) 369-7907
EMAIL: bbcookbook@aol.com • WEBSITE: www.bbcookbook.com

Great Adventures!   Great Food!

Colorado
Bed & Breakfast
Cookbook

Washington State
Bed & Breakfast
Cookbook

Get your copies today!

Order Form for Peppermint Press B & B Cookbooks

Please ask in your local bookstore for the *Washington State Bed & Breakfast Cookbook* or the *Colorado Bed & Breakfast Cookbook*. Or you may order directly from Peppermint Press. Books will be shipped immediately. We accept VISA, MASTERCARD and CHECKS.

Please send me_____copies of the
WASHINGTON STATE BED & BREAKFAST COOKBOOK @ $21.95 each_____
   (Colorado residents add $1.60 tax per book)
   Shipping and handling: Add $3.00 per book   _____
   (Canadian and overseas orders add $10.00 per book for shipping)

Please send me_____copies of the
COLORADO BED & BREAKFAST COOKBOOK @ $18.95 each   _____
   (Colorado residents add $1.38 tax per book)   _____
   Shipping and handling: Add $3.00 per book   _____
   (Canadian and overseas orders add $10.00 per book for shipping)

SAVE! Please send me _____VALUE PACKS* @ $35.00 each   _____
*Each VALUE PACK contains 1 Colorado book and 1 Washington book
   (Colorado residents add $2.56 tax per Value Pack)
   Shipping and handling: Add $5.00 per Value Pack   _____
   (Canadian and overseas orders add $15.00 per Value Pack for shipping)

                                   TOTAL: _____

Please make checks payable to: **Peppermint Press**
(Payable in U.S. dollars only. No C.O.D.'s or Cash.)

Name_____ Street _____

City_____ State____ Zip _____ Tel _____

Please charge to my VISA ____ or MasterCard ____

Card number _____ Exp_____

Cardholder's signature _____

Send order form to:

Peppermint Press • PO Box 370235 • Denver, CO 80237-0235
or

TEL: (800) 758-0803   FAX: (303) 369-7907
EMAIL: bbcookbook@aol.com • WEBSITE: www.bbcookbook.com

Great Adventures!   Great Food!

Colorado Bed & Breakfast Cookbook

Washington State Bed & Breakfast Cookbook

Get your copies today!